AF316645

Essentials of Biostatistics
for Medical Students

(INCLUDING MANUAL ON STATISTICAL ANALYSIS USING SPSS)

Dr. A.B.Ram Jyothis

Professor and Head
Department of Homoeopathic Pharmacy
Athurasramam NSS Homoeopathic Medical College
Sachivothamapuram, Kottayam, Kerala.

INDIA • SINGAPORE • MALAYSIA

This work is dedicated to my Parents, Teachers, and all Students.

Table of Contents

Preface

Welcome to "Essentials of Biostatistics for Medical Students." As the author of this book, I am delighted to present to you a comprehensive guide to the essential concepts, principles, and methods in biostatistics tailored specifically for health sciences. This book is the culmination of my passion for both statistics and medical education, and it is my sincere hope that it will serve as a valuable resource for students of health sciences.

This book aims to simplify biostatistics for medical students, regardless of their mathematical proficiency, by offering clear explanations and practical examples linked to medical research. It strives to prepare students for statistical analysis in their dissertations and short-term research, underlining the importance of statistics in conducting impactful research to arrive at a meaningful conclusion.

The highlight of this book is the inclusion of a manual for statistical analysis using SPSS software and a guide to sample size estimation using G-power. These tools are indispensable for medical students embarking on research endeavours, as they provide practical solutions for conducting statistical analyses efficiently and accurately. The SPSS manual offers step-by-step instructions for performing a wide range of statistical tests and analyses commonly used in medical research, while the G-power guide assists students in determining the appropriate sample size for their studies, thereby enhancing the validity and reliability of their findings.

By mastering the concepts and methods presented in this book, students will be better prepared to design research studies, analyse data, and draw valid conclusions that contribute to the advancement of medical knowledge.

– Dr. A.B. Ram Jyothis

Acknowledgement

I extend my heartfelt gratitude to all who have contributed to the completion of this book, "Essentials of Biostatistics for Medical Students." Your support, guidance, and encouragement have been invaluable throughout this journey.

I am deeply indebted to my esteemed teachers and mentors, particularly Dr. Sandeep Sugathan MD, DPH, FAIMER Fellow, and Dr. Oommen P Mathew PhD, for their invaluable insights and practical applications of biostatistics in medical research. Their expertise and mentorship have shaped my understanding and inspired me to delve deeper into this field.

I also want to express my sincere appreciation to my colleagues and fellow researchers for their support and collaborative spirit. Their feedback and constructive criticism have been instrumental in refining the content of this book and ensuring its relevance to the needs of medical students.

To my students, past and present, I am grateful for your enthusiasm for learning and curiosity about biostatistics. Your engagement and eagerness to explore new concepts have motivated me to create a resource that is accessible and engaging for medical students.

My heartfelt thanks go to my family for their unwavering support and understanding. Their patience, encouragement, and sacrifices have been the cornerstone of my success. I am especially grateful to my spouse – Dr.Lilly and children – Anand and Adithi for their understanding and willingness to share their family time, allowing me to devote myself fully to this project.

Thank you all for your unwavering support, encouragement, and belief in this endeavour.

Chapter 1

Introduction to Biostatistics

Definition and Scope of Biostatistics:

Definition: Biostatistics is a branch of statistics that focuses on the application of statistical methods to biological, health, and medical sciences. It involves the collection, analysis, interpretation, presentation, and organization of data to draw meaningful inferences and make informed decisions in the fields of biology, medicine, and public health.

Scope of Biostatistics:

1. **Data Collection:** Biostatisticians play a crucial role in designing experiments and surveys to collect relevant data in biological and health studies. They develop methods for systematic data collection, ensuring the information gathered is representative and reliable.

2. **Descriptive Statistics:** Biostatistics involves summarizing and describing data using measures such as mean, median, mode, and standard deviation. Descriptive statistics provide a clear and concise overview of the characteristics of a dataset.

3. **Inferential Statistics:** The core of biostatistics lies in making inferences about a population based on a sample of data. Inferential statistics help researchers draw conclusions, estimate parameters, and make predictions with a certain level of confidence.

4. **Hypothesis Testing:** Biostatisticians formulate and test hypotheses to assess the significance of observed differences or associations in biological and health-related phenomena. This process aids in decision-making and supports evidence-based practices.

5. **Experimental Design:** Biostatistics is instrumental in designing experiments, clinical trials, and epidemiological studies. Proper

experimental design ensures that studies are conducted in a way that allows for valid and reliable statistical analysis.

6. **Survival Analysis:** In medical and biological research, biostatisticians employ survival analysis to assess the time until an event of interest occurs. This is particularly relevant in studies related to disease progression, treatment efficacy, and patient outcomes.

7. **Epidemiology:** Biostatistics is extensively used in epidemiological studies to Analyse the distribution and determinants of health-related events in populations. Statistical methods help identify risk factors, trends, and patterns in disease occurrence.

8. **Regression Analysis:** Biostatisticians utilize regression analysis to model relationships between variables, facilitating the identification of predictors and their impact on outcomes. This is essential in understanding complex biological systems and disease processes.

9. **Meta-analysis:** Biostatistics contributes to the synthesis of information from multiple studies through meta-analysis. This approach provides a comprehensive overview of existing evidence, aiding in evidence-based decision-making.

10. **Public Health Decision-Making:** Biostatistics informs public health policies and interventions by providing evidence-based insights. It aids in assessing the effectiveness of public health programs and initiatives.

Importance of biostatistics in medical research

Biostatistics plays a pivotal role in medical research by providing the essential tools and methodologies for collecting, analysing, interpreting, and drawing meaningful conclusions from data in the fields of medicine, biology, and public health. This interdisciplinary field contributes significantly to the advancement of medical knowledge, evidence-based decision-making, and the improvement of healthcare outcomes. In this comprehensive exploration, we delve into the multifaceted importance of biostatistics in medical research, touching upon its role in study design, data analysis, clinical trials, epidemiology, public health, and more.

1. **Fundamental to Study Design:** Biostatistics is foundational to the design of medical studies, ensuring that research endeavours are

conducted with rigor and validity. Biostatisticians contribute to the planning phase by determining sample sizes, randomisation protocols, and methodologies for data collection. The careful consideration of statistical power and significance helps researchers design studies that are capable of detecting meaningful effects, enhancing the reliability of study findings.

2. **Robust Data Analysis:** One of the primary contributions of biostatistics is in the realm of data analysis. It provides researchers with a diverse array of statistical techniques to Analyse complex datasets. Descriptive statistics offer a snapshot of data characteristics, while inferential statistics enable researchers to make predictions and draw conclusions about populations based on sample data. Biostatistical methods such as regression analysis and survival analysis allow for the exploration of relationships between variables and the assessment of time-to-event outcomes, respectively.

3. **Clinical Trials and Drug Development:** In the realm of clinical trials, biostatistics is indispensable. Randomised controlled trials (RCTs) are the gold standard for assessing the efficacy and safety of interventions. Biostatisticians contribute to trial design, ensuring randomisation, blinding, and appropriate statistical analysis methods. They play a crucial role in determining the primary and secondary endpoints, selecting appropriate statistical tests, and implementing strategies to control for confounding variables. Biostatistical analyses of clinical trial data provide the evidence needed for regulatory approval of new drugs and medical interventions.

4. **Epidemiology and Disease Surveillance:** Epidemiology, the study of the distribution and determinants of health-related events in populations, heavily relies on biostatistics. Biostatistical methods are applied to assess the prevalence and incidence of diseases, identify risk factors, and estimate associations between exposures and outcomes. In outbreak investigations, biostatisticians help model the spread of diseases, predict future trends, and evaluate the effectiveness of interventions. Biostatistics also facilitates disease surveillance by analysing patterns of health-related events over time.

5. **Public Health Decision-Making:** Biostatistics plays a key role in informing public health policies and decision-making. Through the

analysis of population-level data, biostatisticians contribute to the identification of health disparities, assessment of health outcomes, and evaluation of the impact of public health interventions. This evidence-based approach helps public health officials make informed decisions regarding resource allocation, disease prevention strategies, and healthcare planning.

6. **Genetic and Genomic Research:** In the era of precision medicine, biostatistics is instrumental in genetic and genomic research. It aids in the analysis of large-scale genetic data, identifying genetic markers associated with diseases, and understanding the genetic basis of complex traits. Biostatistical methods, such as genome-wide association studies (GWAS) and bioinformatics, help researchers unravel the intricate relationship between genetics and health outcomes, paving the way for personalized treatment approaches.

7. **Quality Improvement and Patient Outcomes:** Biostatistics contributes to quality improvement initiatives in healthcare by analysing patient outcomes, assessing the effectiveness of healthcare interventions, and identifying areas for improvement. Through statistical process control and analysis of variation, biostatisticians assist in enhancing the quality and safety of healthcare delivery. They play a role in monitoring patient outcomes, identifying trends, and implementing evidence-based practices to optimize healthcare services.

8. **Health Economics and Cost-Benefit Analysis:** In the context of health economics, biostatistics is employed to assess the economic impact of healthcare interventions. Cost-benefit analysis and cost-effectiveness analysis help policymakers and healthcare administrators make decisions about resource allocation by evaluating the economic efficiency of different healthcare strategies. Biostatistical methods provide a quantitative framework for assessing the value of medical interventions in terms of their impact on health outcomes relative to their costs.

9. **Assessing Treatment Efficacy and Safety:** Biostatistics is integral to assessing the efficacy and safety of medical treatments. Whether analysing data from clinical trials, observational studies, or real-world evidence, biostatisticians employ statistical methods to

determine the effectiveness of treatments, evaluate side effects, and identify potential risks and benefits. This information is crucial for clinicians, regulators, and patients in making informed decisions about treatment options.

10. **Precision Public Health:** The emerging field of precision public health leverages biostatistical methods to tailor interventions to specific population subgroups based on their unique characteristics and risk factors. By analysing large datasets and incorporating information on genetics, environment, and social determinants of health, biostatistics contributes to a more personalized and targeted approach to public health interventions.

11. **Communicating Findings Effectively:** Biostatistics is not just about numbers; it is also about effective communication. Biostatisticians play a crucial role in translating complex statistical findings into comprehensible and actionable information for researchers, clinicians, policymakers, and the general public. Graphical representations, data visualization, and clear explanations of statistical results help bridge the gap between technical analyses and practical applications.

Basic Principles and Concepts of Biostatistics:

Biostatistics is a branch of statistics applied to biological, health, and medical sciences. It involves the application of statistical methods to collect, Analyse, interpret, present, and draw meaningful inferences from biological and health-related data. Understanding the basic principles and concepts of biostatistics is essential for researchers, healthcare professionals, and decision-makers in the fields of medicine and public health.

1. **Descriptive Statistics:** Descriptive statistics summarize and describe the main features of a dataset. Measures such as mean, median, mode, range, and standard deviation provide a concise overview of the central tendency and variability of the data.

2. **Inferential Statistics:** Inferential statistics involve making inferences about a population based on a sample of data. This includes hypothesis testing, confidence intervals, and regression analysis to draw conclusions beyond the observed data.

3. **Population and Sample:** The population refers to the entire group under study, while a sample is a subset of the population. Biostatistics often involves studying a sample to make inferences about the entire population.

4. **Randomisation:** Randomisation is the process of assigning subjects or treatments randomly in a study. It helps eliminate bias and ensures that each participant has an equal chance of being in any experimental group.

5. **Probability:** Probability is the likelihood of an event occurring. It is a fundamental concept in biostatistics used to quantify uncertainty and make informed predictions about outcomes.

6. **Hypothesis Testing:** Hypothesis testing is a statistical method used to evaluate a hypothesis about a population parameter. It involves comparing observed data to what would be expected under a null hypothesis and determining if the observed differences are statistically significant.

7. **Confidence Intervals:** Confidence intervals provide a range within which the true population parameter is likely to fall with a certain level of confidence. They offer a more informative estimate than point estimates alone.

8. **Measures of Association:** Measures of association quantify the strength and direction of relationships between variables. Common measures include correlation coefficients, odds ratios, and relative risks.

9. **Regression Analysis:** Regression analysis assesses the relationship between a dependent variable and one or more independent variables. It helps predict the value of the dependent variable based on the values of the independent variables.

10. **Experimental Design:** Experimental design involves planning and organizing studies to ensure valid and reliable results. Randomisation, blinding, and control groups are essential components of well-designed experiments.

11. **Statistical Significance vs. Clinical Significance:** Statistical significance indicates whether observed differences are likely due to chance. Clinical significance, on the other hand, assesses the practical importance or relevance of observed effects in a real-world context.

12. **P-values:** P-values indicate the probability of obtaining observed results or more extreme results if the null hypothesis is true. A smaller p-value suggests stronger evidence against the null hypothesis.

13. **Null Hypothesis and Alternative Hypothesis:** The null hypothesis (H0) posits that there is no effect or no difference, while the alternative hypothesis (H1) suggests the presence of an effect or difference. Hypothesis testing aims to determine which hypothesis is more plausible based on the data.

14. **Bias and Variability:** Bias refers to systematic errors in study design, data collection, or analysis that led to incorrect conclusions. Variability, on the other hand, is the natural fluctuation in data points. Both must be considered in the interpretation of study results.

15. **Variables :** A variable is any characteristic, trait, or attribute that can take on different values. Variables are crucial components in the study of phenomena, and their types depend on how they can be measured or categorized. The main types of variables are –

    a) **Independent Variable:** The independent variable, also known as the predictor or explanatory variable, is manipulated, or controlled in an experiment. It is believed to influence the dependent variable. Changes in the independent variable are hypothesized to cause changes in the dependent variable.

    b) **Dependent Variable:** The dependent variable, also known as the response or outcome variable, is what researchers measure in the study. It is considered the effect or outcome that may be influenced by changes in the independent variable.

    c) **Discrete Variable:** Discrete variables take on distinct, separate values. These values are often counted and are finite or countably infinite. Examples include the number of children in a family, the number of cars in a parking lot, or the outcomes of tossing a coin.

    d) **Continuous Variable:** Continuous variables can take on any value within a given range and can be measured with great precision. Examples include height, weight, temperature, and time. Continuous variables are often measured using real numbers.

    e) **Categorical Variable:** Categorical variables represent categories or groups. They are often qualitative and can be nominal or ordinal. Nominal categories have no inherent order (e.g., colours, gender), while ordinal categories have a meaningful order (e.g., education levels, socio-economic status).

I. **Nominal Variable:** Nominal variables are categorical variables with no inherent order among categories. Examples include gender, ethnicity, or types of fruits. These variables are used for classification purposes.

II. **Ordinal Variable:** Ordinal variables are categorical variables with a meaningful order among categories. However, the intervals between the categories are not equal. Examples include education levels, income brackets, or satisfaction ratings.

f) **Ratio Variable:** Ratio variables have a true zero point, meaning that zero represents the complete absence of the variable. Examples include height, weight, income, and age. Ratio variables allow for meaningful ratios and mathematical operations.

g) **Interval Variable:** Interval variables have equal intervals between values, but they lack a true zero point. Temperature measured in Celsius or Fahrenheit is an example. While differences between values are meaningful, ratios are not. For instance, 20 degrees Celsius is not twice as hot as 10 degrees Celsius.

h) **Extraneous (confounding) Variable:** – Extraneous variables are unwanted variables in a study that can affect the relationship between the independent and dependent variables. They are often controlled or considered in research to prevent confounding effects.

i) **Moderating Variable:** – A moderating variable influences the strength or direction of the relationship between the independent and dependent variables. It helps identify conditions under which the relationship may be stronger or weaker.

Chapter 2

Data Presentation in Biostatistics

Definition and types of data

In medical research, data refer to the information collected through various methods, including observations, measurements, or experiments. This raw information serves as the foundation for analysis, interpretation, and drawing conclusions in the field of medicine. Understanding the types of data is crucial for selecting appropriate statistical techniques and deriving meaningful insights from research findings.

Types of Data:

1. **Qualitative Data:** Qualitative data are non-numerical and represent attributes or characteristics. They provide information about qualities and cannot be measured in terms of quantity.
   Examples: Patient satisfaction ratings, diagnostic categories (e.g., presence or absence of a symptom), or qualitative descriptors of pain (e.g., mild, moderate, severe).

2. **Quantitative Data:** Quantitative data are numerical and represent measurable quantities. They provide information about the amount or magnitude of a phenomenon.
   Examples: Laboratory test results (e.g., blood glucose levels), vital signs (e.g., heart rate, blood pressure), or patient age.

3. **Discrete Data:** Discrete data consist of individual, separate values with no intermediate values. They often represent counts or whole numbers.
   Examples: Number of hospital admissions, count of adverse events, or the number of individuals in a study group.

4. **Continuous Data:** Continuous data can take any value within a given range and can be measured with great precision. They often require real numbers for representation.
   Examples: Height, weight, serum cholesterol levels, or duration of treatment.

5. **Nominal Data:** Nominal data are categorical variables with no inherent order or ranking among categories. They are used for classification purposes.
   Examples: Types of diseases (e.g., diabetes, hypertension), gender, or types of medical procedures.

6. **Ordinal Data:** Ordinal data are categorical variables with a meaningful order among categories, but the intervals between them are not equal.
   Examples: Patient satisfaction levels (e.g., very satisfied, satisfied, dissatisfied), stages of disease severity, or clinical severity ratings.

7. **Ratio Data:** Ratio data have a true zero point, representing the absence of the variable. They allow for meaningful ratios and mathematical operations.
   Examples: Patient age, body mass index (BMI), blood pressure measurements, or laboratory values with a true zero point.

8. **Interval Data:** Interval data have equal intervals between values, but they lack a true zero point. Ratios are not meaningful in interval data.
   Examples: Temperature measured in Celsius or Fahrenheit, pain intensity ratings on a scale, or scores on standardized assessments.

9. **Categorical Data:** Categorical data include both nominal and ordinal variables. They represent categories rather than numerical values.
   Examples: Types of medications prescribed, blood groups, or types of surgical interventions.

10. **Numerical Data:** Numerical data include both discrete and continuous variables. They represent measurable quantities.
    Examples: Laboratory values (e.g., white blood cell count, serum creatinine), heart rate measurements, or disease incidence rates.

11. **Binary Data:** Binary data are a special case of categorical data with only two categories, often represented as 0 and 1.

    Examples: Presence or absence of a specific symptom, success or failure of a treatment, or positive/negative diagnostic test results.

12. **Time-Series Data:** Time-series data are observations or measurements collected over time, providing information on trends, patterns, and changes in variables.

    Examples: Longitudinal patient data, monitoring disease progression over time, or assessing treatment outcomes at multiple time points.

Methods of data presentation

Effective data presentation is crucial in medical research to convey research findings clearly, facilitate understanding, and support evidence-based decision-making. Two method of data presentation are.

- **Tabular presentation**
- **Diagrammatic presentation**

- **Tabular presentation**: It is a common way to present information in a structured and organized manner. It is especially useful in medical research where data is often complex and voluminous. Tables are used to present numerical data, textural data, and matrix data. They can be used to compare different groups of data, show trends over time, and highlight important findings. When creating tables, it is important to follow certain rules to ensure that they are clear and easy to read. Tables should have a clear title, column headings, and row labels. Data should be presented in a logical and consistent manner, and any abbreviations or symbols used should be explained in a footnote.

  Examples of how tables can be used in medical research:

  - Clinical trial results: Tables can be used to present the results of clinical trials, including the number of participants, treatment groups, and outcomes.

- o Epidemiological studies: Tables can be used to present the incidence and prevalence of diseases in different populations, as well as risk factors and other relevant data.
- o Laboratory research: Tables can be used to present the results of laboratory experiments, including measurements, observations, and other data.
- o Systematic reviews and meta-analyses: Tables can be used to summarize the results of multiple studies, including study characteristics, outcomes, and effect sizes.

- **Diagrammatic presentation:** Diagrammatic presentation of data is a method of presenting information in a visual format. It is often used in medical research to present complex data in an easy-to-understand manner. Diagrams can be used to represent data in a variety of ways, including bar charts, pie charts, Line charts, Frequency curve, histograms, Box and whisker plots and scatter plots.

Bar charts: They are particularly effective for representing categorical data and making comparisons between different groups or categories. Essential features of bar diagrams are.

- Comparing quantities
- Illustrating trends over time
- Displaying frequency distributions
- Representing survey results
- Highlighting disparities and discrepancies
- Comparing multiple data sets
- Ranking and order
- Presenting proportions and percentages
- Visualizing project timelines
- Comparing performance metrics
- Educational tools

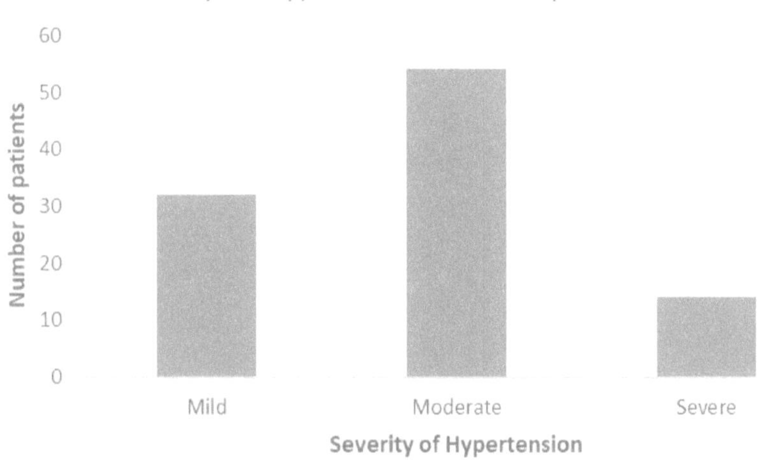

▲ Bar chart : Number of patients with mild, moderate, and severe hypertension

Pie charts: Pie charts are circular statistical graphics that are particularly useful for representing proportional data. They are effective in conveying the distribution of a whole into its constituent parts. The essential features of pie charts are.

- Showing proportions of a whole.
- Comparing percentages.
- Visualizing composition.
- Representing percent distribution.
- Highlighting dominant categories.
- Displaying slices as ratios.
- Comparing few categories.
- Conveying simple data relationships.
- Visualizing survey responses.
- Displaying share of a market.
- Highlighting patterns in data.
- Comparing categories over time.

Distribution of subjects according to blood groups

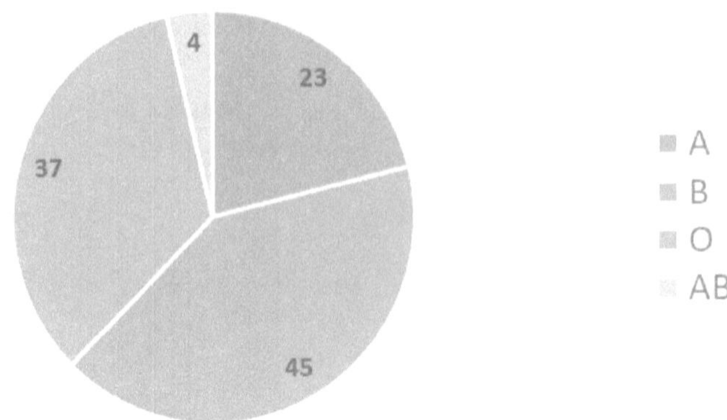

▲ Pie chart : Blood group distribution

Line charts: Line charts are a powerful tool for visualizing data trends and relationships. The essential features of line charts are.

- Time series analysis
- Comparing trends
- Showing progression
- Highlighting patterns
- Correlation analysis
- Forecasting trends
- Monitoring changes
- Displaying averages
- Quality control
- Project management

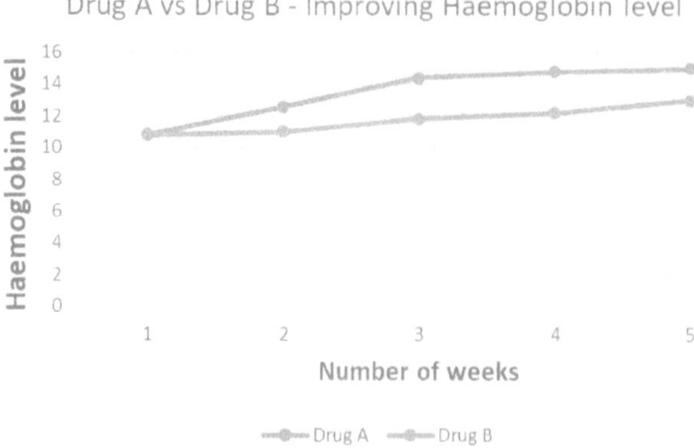

▲ Line chart :Comparative Analysis of Haemoglobin Improvement: Drug A vs. Drug B

Frequency curve: Frequency curve also known as a frequency distribution curve is a graphical representation of the distribution of data points in a dataset. The essential features of line charts are.

- Data Visualization
- Identifying Central Tendency
- Dispersion and Spread
- Skewness and Symmetry
- Outlier Detection
- Comparison of Distributions

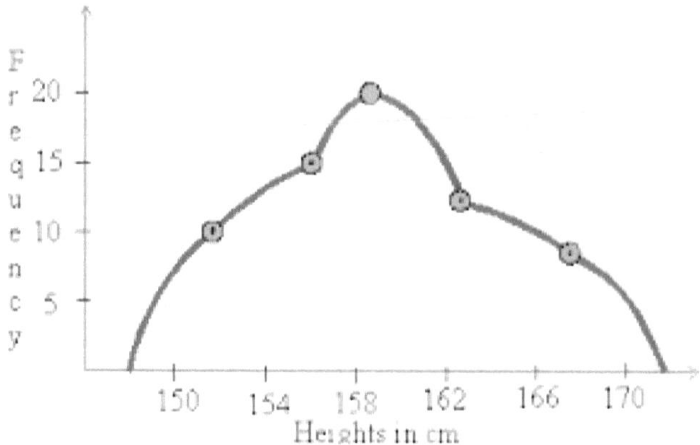

▲ Frequency curve – Distribution of individuals according to height

Scatter diagram: A scatter diagram, also known as a scatter plot, is a type of graphical representation that displays the relationship between two continuous variables. It consists of individual data points, each representing the value of one variable on the horizontal (x-axis) and the corresponding value of the other variable on the vertical (y-axis). The essential features of scatter diagrams are.

- Exploring Relationships
- Correlation Analysis
- Regression Analysis
- Forecasting and Prediction
- Quality Control and Process Improvement
- Risk Assessment and Decision Making
- Experimental Design and Analysis
- Data Exploration and Presentation

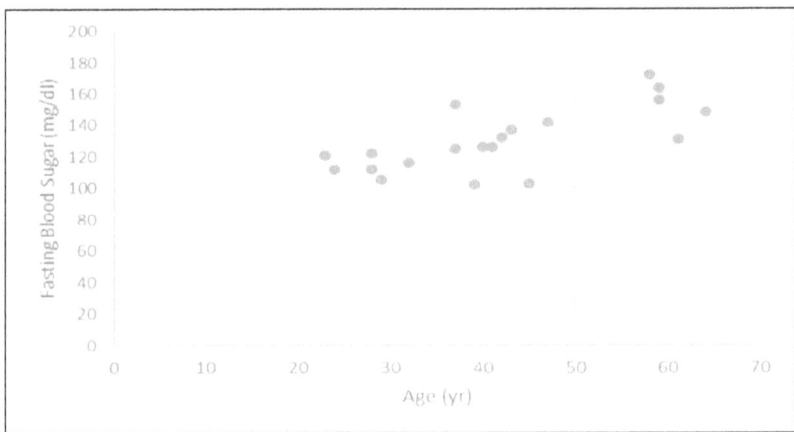

▲ Scatter diagram: Relationship between Age and Fasting Blood Sugar.

Box and whisker plot: A box and whisker plot, also known as a box plot, is a graphical representation of the distribution of a dataset along with its central tendency and variability. It displays key summary statistics such as the median, quartiles, and potential outliers in a compact and visually intuitive manner. The essential features of box and whisker plots are,

- Visualizing Distribution
- Identifying Central Tendency

- Assessing Variability
- Detecting Outliers
- Comparing Groups or Categories
- Monitoring Changes Over Time

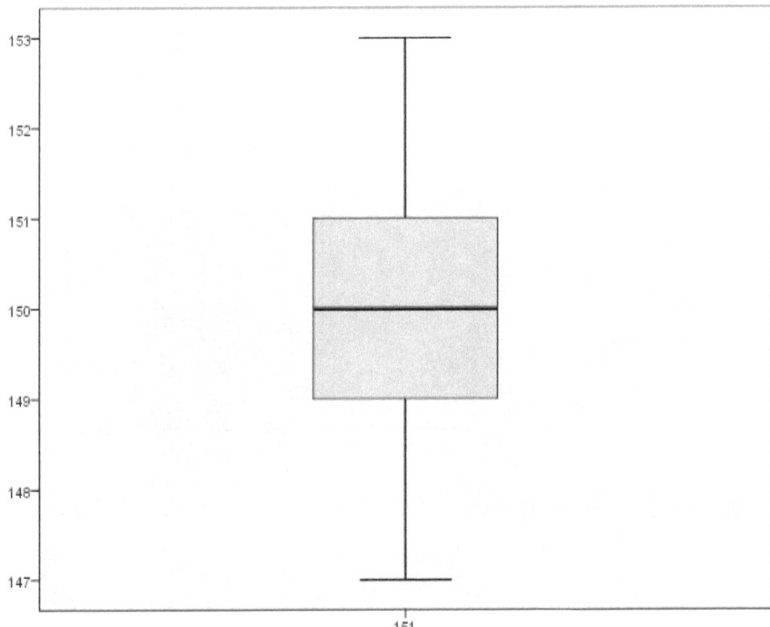

▲ Box and whisker plot : Distribution of Fasting blood sugar of 20 diabetic patients.

Histogram: A histogram is a graphical representation of the distribution of a dataset, particularly for continuous or interval data. It consists of a series of adjacent rectangles (bars) whose heights represent the frequency or relative frequency of observations falling within each interval or bin.

- Visualizing Distribution
- Assessing Central Tendency and Variability
- Identifying Outliers
- Comparing Distributions
- Detecting Patterns and Trends
- Data Preprocessing and Exploration

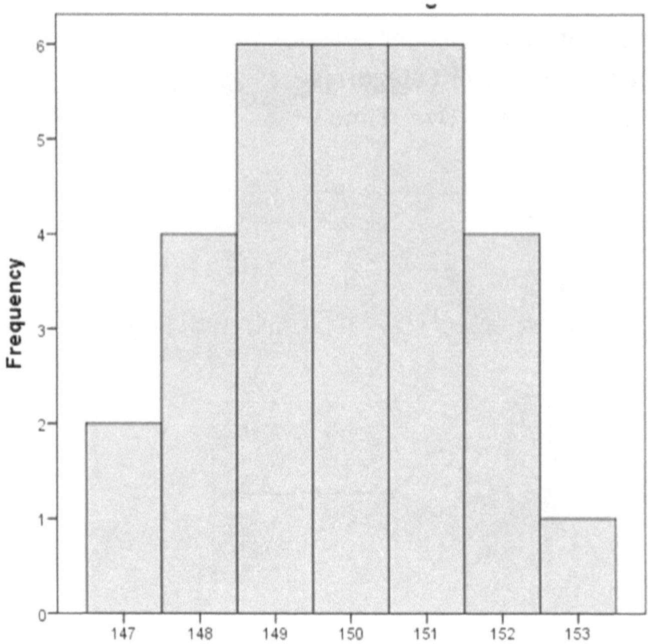

▲ Histogram: Normal distribution of fasting blood sugar of 20 diabetic patients

Chapter 3

Descriptive Statistics

Descriptive statistics is a branch of statistical analysis that involves the collection, presentation, and interpretation of data in a meaningful and informative way. Its primary purpose is to summarise and describe essential features of a dataset, providing a clear and concise overview that facilitates a better understanding of the underlying patterns and characteristics.

The fundamental goal of descriptive statistics is to distil complex datasets into simpler, manageable forms, making it easier for researchers, analysts, and decision-makers to draw insights and make informed decisions. This branch of statistics employs various measures, graphical representations, and numerical summaries to describe the central tendency, dispersion, and shape of a dataset.

Classifications of Descriptive Statistics:

Descriptive statistics can be broadly classified into two main categories: measures of central tendency and measures of dispersion.

1. **Measures of Central Tendency:**

   - **Mean (Average):** The sum of all values divided by the number of observations, providing a measure of the dataset's central value.

     - The **geometric mean** is calculated by multiplying all the values in a dataset and then taking the nth root of the product, where n is the number of values.

     - The **trimmed mean** is a measure of central tendency that is calculated by excluding a certain percentage of the smallest and largest values in a dataset and then calculating the mean of the remaining values. It is a way to reduce the impact of outliers or extreme values on the mean.

- The **weighted mean** is a measure of central tendency where different values in the dataset are assigned different weights based on their importance or significance. Each value is multiplied by its corresponding weight, and the sum of these products is divided by the sum of the weights.

- **Median:** The middle value in a dataset when arranged in ascending or descending order, representing the central position.
- **Mode:** The most frequently occurring value in a dataset.

Measure	Application	Example
Mean	The average value in a data set. Used to compare groups or assess changes over time.	The mean age of patients with diabetes in a study is 52 years.
Median	The middle value in a data set. Used to describe the typical value or the central tendency of skewed data.	The median survival time of patients with lung cancer in a trial is 18 months.
Mode	The most frequently occurring value(s) in a data set. Used to describe the most common category or outcome.	The mode of blood group among donors in a blood bank is O.

2. **Measures of Dispersion:**

- **Range:** The difference between the maximum and minimum values in a dataset, indicating the spread of the data.
- **Variance:** The average of the squared deviations of the data values from the mean. It measures how far the data values are from the mean, but it is not in the same unit as the data.
- **Mean deviation:** The average of the absolute deviations of the data values from the mean. It measures how much the data values differ from the mean, and it is in the same unit as the data. It is less affected by outliers than the standard deviation, but it is more difficult to calculate.

- **Standard Deviation:** The square root of the variance, offering a more interpretable measure of the spread of data.
- **Interquartile range (IQR):** It is defined as the difference between the 75th and 25th percentiles of the data, or equivalently, the difference between the third and first quartiles. The IQR contains the middle 50% of the data values, and it is not affected by outliers or extreme values.
- **Coefficient of variance (CV):** It is calculated by dividing the standard deviation by the mean and multiplying by 100 to express it as a percentage. The CV is also known as the relative standard deviation (RSD). The CV is useful for comparing the variability of different data sets that have different units or scales. A lower CV indicates less variability or more consistency, while a higher CV indicates more variability or less consistency.

Measures of central tendency and dispersion are useful tools to summarize and analyse data in medical statistics. They can help to:

- Describe the typical or average value of a variable, such as the mean, median, or mode.
- Compare different groups or populations, such as the difference in mean blood pressure between men and women.
- Assess the variability or spread of a variable, such as the standard deviation, range, or interquartile range.
- Detect outliers or extreme values that may indicate errors or anomalies in the data, such as using boxplots or z-scores.

Normal distribution and its importance

A normal distribution is a theoretical distribution of values that is symmetric, bell-shaped, and determined by two parameters: the mean and the standard deviation. The mean is the centre of the distribution, and the standard deviation is a measure of how spread out the values are. In a normal distribution, about 68% of the values are within one standard deviation of the mean, 95% are within two standard deviations, and 99.7% are within three standard deviations.

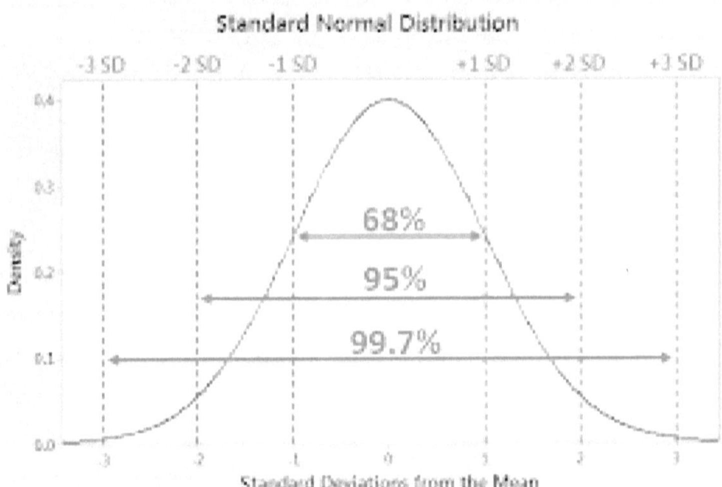

Normal distributions are important in statistics because they are often used to model natural and social phenomena, such as height, weight, blood pressure, IQ, test scores, etc. Many statistical tests and methods assume that the data follow a normal distribution, or at least are compatible with it.

Some of the characteristics of normal distribution are.

- It is symmetric, unimodal, and bell-shaped.
- The mean, median, and mode are all equal and located at the centre of the curve.
- The area under the curve is equal to 1 or 100%.
- The curve is determined by two parameters: the mean and the standard deviation.
- The curve is denser in the centre and less dense in the tails.

Skewness

Skewess is a measure of the asymmetry of a distribution. A distribution is asymmetrical when its left and right side are not mirror images. A distribution can have right (or positive), left (or negative), or zero skewness. Skewness indicates how the data deviates from a perfectly symmetrical distribution, such as a normal distribution.

The three types of skewness are.

Right skew (also called positive skew): A right-skewed distribution is longer on the right side of its peak than on its left. This means that the majority of data points are concentrated on the left side of the distribution, and there are some extreme values on the right side. In a right-skewed distribution, the mean is greater than the median and the mode: Mean > Median > Mode.

Left skew (also called negative skew): A left-skewed distribution is longer on the left side of its peak than on its right. This means that the majority of data points are concentrated on the right side of the distribution, and there are some extreme values on the left side. In a left-skewed distribution, the mean is less than the median and the mode: Mean < Median < Mode.

Zero skew: When a distribution has zero skew, it is symmetrical. Its left and right sides are mirror images. Normal distributions have zero skew, but they're not the only distributions with zero skew. Any symmetrical distribution, such as a uniform distribution or some bimodal distributions, will also have zero skew. In a distribution with zero skew, the mean and median are equal: Mean = Median = Mode

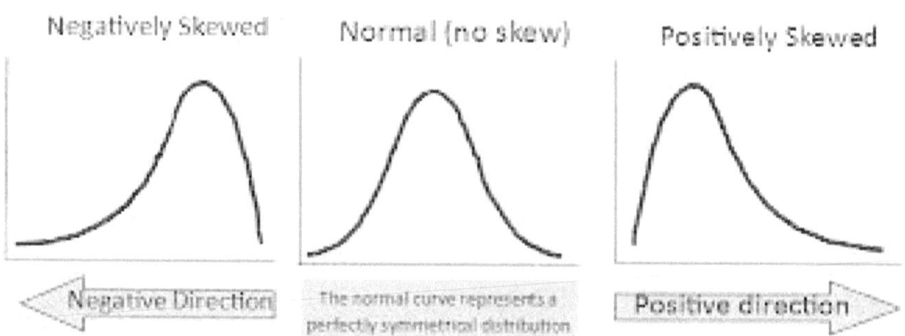

Kurtosis

Kurtosis is a measure of how often outliers occur in a distribution. Outliers are values that are very high or very low compared to the mean. There are three types of kurtoses –

- **Mesokurtic**: A distribution is considered mesokurtic when it has kurtosis equal to the normal distribution (which has a kurtosis of 0). Mesokurtic distributions have a similar shape to the normal distribution, with moderate tails and a moderate peak.
- **Leptokurtic**: A distribution is leptokurtic when it has positive kurtosis, meaning it has fatter tails and a sharper peak compared to the normal distribution. Leptokurtic distributions exhibit more extreme values and higher peakness in the centre.
- **Platykurtic**: A distribution is platykurtic when it has negative kurtosis, indicating thinner tails and a flatter peak compared to the normal distribution. Platykurtic distributions have a more spread-out shape, with fewer extreme values and a less pronounced central peak.

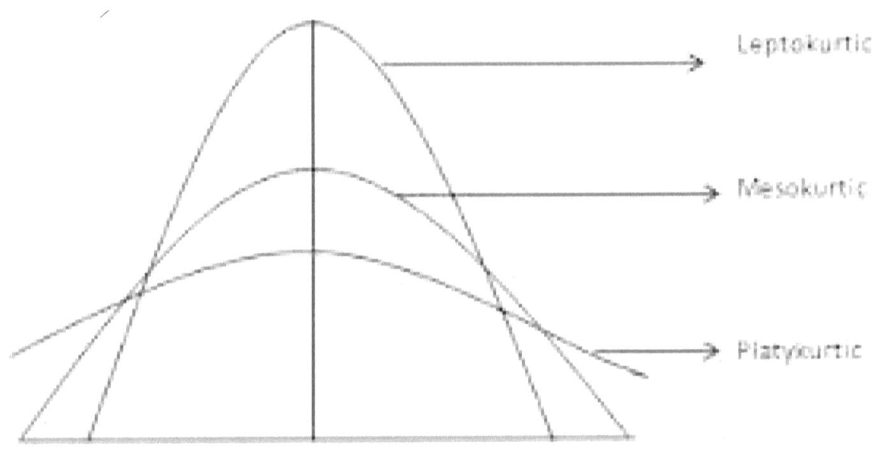

Skewness and kurtosis in medical research aid in assessing data distribution, identifying outliers, and guiding statistical test selection. They inform researchers about normality assumptions, supporting quality control and influencing risk assessments. Understanding these measures enhances the accuracy and reliability of findings in health-related studies.

Conditions for Normal distributions

Evidence of a normal distribution in data can be assessed through visual inspection, statistical tests, and practical considerations. Here are some common methods:

1. **Histogram or Frequency Plot:** Visualizing the data through a histogram can provide a quick visual indication of whether the distribution is approximately normal. A bell-shaped curve suggests normality.

2. **Q-Q Plot (Quantile-Quantile Plot):** A Q-Q plot compares the quantiles of the observed data against the quantiles of a theoretical normal distribution. If the points closely follow a straight line, it suggests normality.

3. **Shapiro-Wilk Test:** A statistical test like the Shapiro-Wilk test can formally assess whether the data follows a normal distribution. A p-value greater than the significance level (e.g., 0.05) suggests the data is normally distributed.

4. **Kurtosis and Skewness:** Calculating skewness and kurtosis can provide numerical measures of the symmetry and shape of the distribution. Values close to 0 indicate normality.

5. **Central Limit Theorem:** If the sample size is sufficiently large, the central limit theorem suggests that the distribution of the sample mean will be approximately normal, regardless of the original distribution of the data.

6. **Empirical Rule (68-95-99.7 Rule):** In a normal distribution, approximately 68% of the data falls within one standard deviation of the mean, 95% within two standard deviations, and 99.7% within three standard deviations.

7. **Parametric Tests:** When conducting hypothesis tests or confidence intervals, assuming normality may be appropriate. For example, t-tests and ANOVA assume normal distributions.

It's important to note that real-world data may not always perfectly follow a normal distribution. In practice, these methods are used to assess the degree of approximation to normality and to make informed decisions about statistical analyses. Multiple methods and a combination of visual and statistical approaches are often used for a comprehensive evaluation.

Other types of distributions in statistics

1. **Binomial Distribution:** Describes the number of successes in a fixed number of independent Bernoulli trials, each with the same probability of success.

2. **Poisson Distribution:** Models the number of events that occur in a fixed interval of time or space, given a known average rate of occurrence.

3. **Uniform Distribution:** All outcomes have equal probability. The probability density function is constant within a specified range.

4. **Exponential Distribution:** Describes the time between events in a Poisson process. It has a memoryless property, meaning future events are independent of the past.

5. **Log-Normal Distribution:** The logarithm of the variable is normally distributed, resulting in a skewed distribution when the variable itself is positive.

6. **Gamma Distribution:** Generalizes the exponential distribution and includes as special cases the exponential, Erlang, and chi-squared distributions.

7. **Beta Distribution:** Describes the distribution of random variables limited to intervals (0, 1). It is often used in Bayesian statistics.

8. **Cauchy Distribution:** Has heavy tails and no defined mean or variance. Commonly used in physics and engineering.

9. **Student's t-Distribution:** Arises in the estimation of the mean of a normally distributed population when the sample size is small.

These distributions have various applications in different fields, and their characteristics influence statistical analyses and modelling approaches. The choice of distribution depends on the nature of the data and the specific requirements of the analysis.

Chapter 4

Study Designs in Medical Research

Observational studies

Observational studies are a type of research that involves collecting and analysing data from a sample of individuals without manipulating or intervening in their natural settings. Observational studies can be used to describe the characteristics, behaviours, and outcomes of a population, or to explore the associations between exposures and outcomes. Observational studies can also provide evidence for causal inference, although they are more prone to confounding and bias than experimental studies.

Observational studies can be broadly classified into two main types based on their designs and objectives: **Descriptive studies** and **Analytical studies** .Each type has its own advantages and disadvantages, depending on the research question, the availability of data, and the ethical and practical issues involved.

Descriptive studies

- **Case Series and Case Reports:** Describing the characteristics and outcomes of individuals with a specific condition, these studies lack comparison groups but offer valuable insights. Case reports offer valuable insights into rare or unusual medical conditions, providing detailed descriptions of individual cases and aiding in the identification of new diseases or treatment approaches. They serve as the initial documentation of novel observations, contributing to medical knowledge and informing clinical practice. However, case reports lack generalisability and cannot establish causality or determine prevalence due to their focus on individual cases and absence of comparison groups.

- **Ecological Studies:** Analysing population-level data, ecological studies investigate associations between exposures and outcomes at a group or community level. They are useful for generating hypotheses and identifying potential public health trends. However, ecological studies face challenges in establishing causal relationships, as they may be prone to the ecological fallacy and lack individual-level data, limiting their ability to account for confounding factors.

- **Cross-Sectional Study:** A cross-sectional study is a research design that involves the collection of data from a population or a representative subset at a single point in time. The primary objective is to capture a snapshot of the characteristics, behaviours, or conditions of the study subjects at a specific moment. Cross-sectional studies are useful for assessing the prevalence of a particular outcome or exposure within a population. However, they do not establish cause-and-effect relationships and are more focused on describing the distribution of variables at a specific time.

Analytical studies

- **Case-control studies**: These studies compare individuals with a specific outcome (cases) to those without the outcome (controls), retrospectively assessing exposures to identify associations and potential risk factors. Case-control studies are efficient for investigating rare outcomes, providing a cost-effective and quick approach to explore potential associations and generate hypotheses. However, their retrospective design introduces challenges such as recall bias and difficulties in establishing causation. The selection of appropriate controls, potential for bias, and the temporal ambiguity in assessing exposures and outcomes are limitations that require careful consideration in the interpretation of findings.

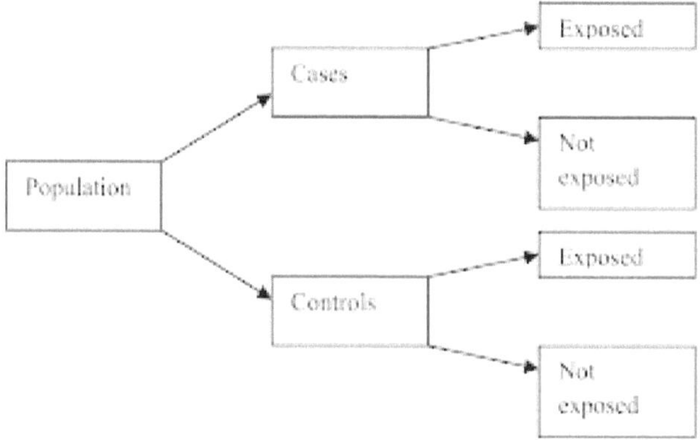

Cohort Study:

A cohort study is a longitudinal observational study that follows a group of individuals (cohort) over an extended period. The cohort is typically categorized based on exposure status, and researchers assess the development of outcomes over time. Cohort studies allow for the examination of the temporal relationship between exposures and outcomes and are particularly useful in determining causation. Cohorts can be prospective (followed forward in time from the present) or retrospective (using historical data).

Types of Cohort study designs:

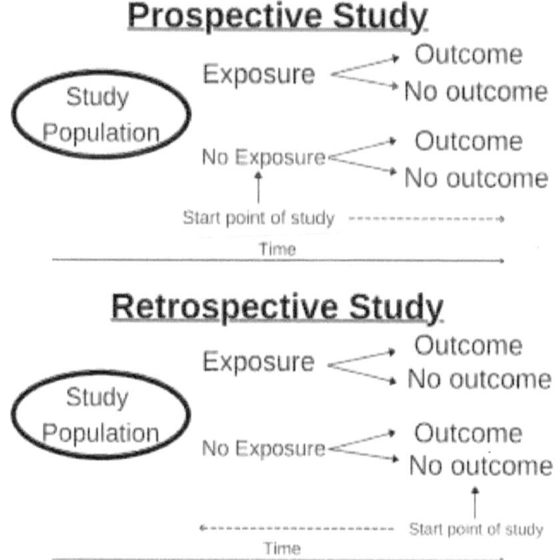

Other designs in cohort study

Nested case-control study	Case-cohort study
Embedded within a cohort study	A type of cohort study
Uses a subset of cases and controls from the cohort	Uses a random sample of the cohort as the control group
Can estimate the relative risk	Can only estimate the hazard ratio
Can control for confounding by matching	Cannot control for confounding by matching
Requires a different control group for each outcome 	Can use the same control group for multiple outcome. 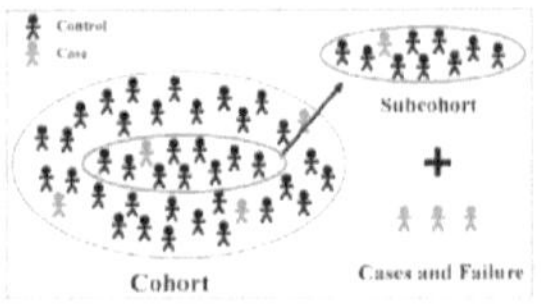

The following table summarises some of the key features and differences of these two types of analytical studies.

Type	Definition	Advantages	Disadvantages
Case-control	A study that compares the exposure history of individuals who have a specific outcome (cases) with those who do not have the outcome (controls).	Efficient and economical for rare outcomes. Can examine multiple exposures for a single outcome. Can study outcomes with long latency periods.	Cannot estimate the incidence or prevalence of an outcome in a population. Prone to selection bias, recall bias, and confounding. May not reflect the exposure distribution in the source population.

Type	Definition	Advantages	Disadvantages
Cohort	A study that follows a group of individuals who share a common exposure or characteristic over time and measures their outcomes.	Can establish the temporal sequence and causality between exposure and outcome. Can estimate the incidence and risk of an outcome in a population. Can examine multiple outcomes for a single exposure.	Time-consuming and costly to conduct. Prone to loss to follow-up and attrition bias. May not be feasible or ethical for rare or harmful exposures.

Experimental studies

Experimental studies are research investigations designed to explore cause-and-effect relationships between variables. In an experimental study, the researcher deliberately manipulates one or more independent variables to observe the impact on a dependent variable, while also attempting to control for other factors that could influence the results. The goal is to establish a causal relationship between the manipulated variables and the observed outcomes. Experimental studies are often considered the gold standard for establishing causation in scientific research.

True Experimental Studies:

Randomised Controlled Trials (RCTs): Participants are randomly assigned to either an experimental group or a control group. The experimental group receives the treatment or intervention, while the control group does not. Randomisation helps control for confounding variables, enhancing internal validity. The key components and characteristics of Randomised Controlled Trials are.

- **Random Assignment:** Participants are randomly assigned to either the experimental group or the control group. Randomisation helps ensure that each group is comparable at the outset, minimizing the likelihood of systematic biases.

  - **Experimental Group:** This is the group that receives the treatment, intervention, or experimental condition under investigation. The purpose is to assess the impact of the intervention on the participants.
  - **Control Group:** This is the group that does not receive the experimental treatment. Instead, they may receive a placebo or standard treatment. The control group serves as a baseline for comparison to evaluate the true effect of the intervention.
  - **Blinding (Single-blind or Double-blind):** To prevent biases in the assessment of outcomes, RCTs often incorporate blinding. In a single-blind study, participants are unaware of whether they are in the experimental or control group. In a double-blind study, both participants and researchers are unaware of group assignments.
  - **Placebo Control:** In medical RCTs, a placebo control may be used in the control group to account for the psychological effects of receiving a treatment. This helps ensure that any observed effects are due to the active ingredients of the intervention, not just the belief in its effectiveness.
  - **Outcome Measures:** RCTs use predefined and standardized outcome measures to assess the impact of the intervention. These measures are chosen based on the research question and are applied consistently across groups.
  - **Randomisation Methods:** Various methods can be used for random assignment, such as computer-generated random numbers or randomisation tables. The goal is to achieve balance between groups, making them comparable in terms of potential confounding variables.

- **Pre-test Post-test Control Group Design:** Participants are randomly assigned to experimental and control groups, and both groups are tested before and after the intervention. This design helps measure the change in the dependent variable and control for individual differences.

Quasi-Experimental Studies:

- **Non-equivalent Control Group Design:** Similar to true experimental design, but participants are not randomly assigned. Instead, pre-existing groups are used, and efforts are made to match them as closely as possible.
- **Time Series Design:** Data is collected over multiple time points before and after the intervention, allowing researchers to examine trends and changes over time.

These classifications highlight the variety of experimental study designs available to researchers, each suited to different research questions and practical constraints. The choice of design depends on the specific objectives of the study, ethical considerations, and the available resources. Experimental studies aim to provide robust evidence for causal relationships between variables, contributing to our understanding of scientific phenomena.

Table that summarises the main differences between true experimental design and quasi-experimental design :

True experimental design	Quasi-experimental design
Participants are randomly assigned to groups.	Participants are assigned to groups based on non-random criteria.
The researcher has control over the intervention.	The researcher often studies pre-existing groups that received different interventions.
There is always a control group.	A control group is not always present.
There is no room for confounding variables.	Confounding variables may affect the results.
It provides the highest level of evidence.	It provides a lower level of evidence than a true experiment.

Table of reporting guidelines for main study types

Study type	Reporting guideline
Randomised controlled trials.	CONSORT
Systematic reviews and meta-analyses	PRISMA
Observational studies	STROBE
Case reports	CARE
Qualitative research	COREQ
Pre-clinical animal studies	ARRIVE
Clinical trials protocols	SPIRIT

Source: https://www.equator-network.org/

Research design considerations and biases.

Medical research is a field of scientific inquiry that aims to advance our understanding of health and disease, ultimately leading to improved patient outcomes. However, the success of medical research hinges on meticulous research design and a keen awareness of potential biases that can impact the validity and reliability of findings. The key considerations inherent in the design of medical research studies are.

Study Objectives and Hypotheses: Clearly defining the objectives and hypotheses is fundamental in medical research. Whether investigating a new treatment, assessing risk factors, or exploring disease mechanisms, a well-defined research question guides subsequent design decisions.

Study Population and Sampling: The selection of an appropriate study population is crucial. Researchers must carefully consider inclusion and exclusion criteria to ensure the relevance and generalisability of the findings. Randomised controlled trials (RCTs) are often employed to minimise selection bias.

Control Groups and Randomisation: In experimental studies, the use of control groups helps establish causation by isolating the effects of the intervention. Randomisation ensures that participants are assigned to treatment and control groups in a way that minimises potential confounding variables.

Blinding and Placebo Control: Employing blinding techniques, such as double-blind or single-blind methodologies, reduces bias by preventing both participants and researchers from knowing the treatment assignments. Placebo control groups help assess the true efficacy of a new intervention.

Ethical Considerations: Medical research must adhere to strict ethical guidelines. Informed consent, confidentiality, and the responsible conduct of research are paramount. Researchers must also consider the potential benefits and risks to participants.

Research biases in medical research:

Research biases in medical research can occur at different stages of the research process, influencing the outcomes and conclusions of studies. Understanding these biases and implementing measures to minimise their impact is crucial for ensuring the validity and reliability of medical research. Here are examples of biases at various stages:

1. **Study Design Stage:**

   - **Selection Bias:** In a clinical trial for a new drug, if participants are recruited exclusively from a single demographic or geographical area, the results may not be applicable to a broader population.
   - **Healthy Volunteer Bias**: If individuals who volunteer for a study are generally healthier than the average population, the study's findings may overestimate the treatment's effectiveness and underestimate potential risks.

2. **Data Collection Stage:**

   - **Recall Bias**: In a case-control study investigating the association between a medication and a rare adverse effect, participants with the adverse effect may have difficulty recalling their medication history accurately, leading to biased results.
   - **Observer Bias**: In a clinical trial evaluating a new surgical procedure, if the surgeons are aware of the treatment group assignments, their assessments of postoperative outcomes may be influenced, leading to biased conclusions.

3. **Data Analysis Stage:**

- **Publication Bias**: A meta-analysis on the effectiveness of a specific treatment may show a skewed positive effect if studies with negative or neutral results are less likely to be published, creating an incomplete and potentially biased evidence base.
- **Funding Bias**: In a study funded by a pharmaceutical company to evaluate the efficacy of its drug, there may be a tendency to emphasize positive outcomes while downplaying or not fully reporting negative results, introducing bias into the data analysis.

4. **Interpretation and Reporting Stage:**

- **Confounding Bias**: In a study examining the relationship between coffee consumption and heart health, if the researchers fail to account for confounding factors like smoking or exercise, the reported association may be confounded and misleading.
- **Length Time Bias**: In a cancer screening program, if the screening method predominantly detects slow-growing tumours, the perceived effectiveness of early detection may be overestimated, as more aggressive tumours may be missed.

Awareness of these biases and their potential impact is essential for researchers to implement appropriate methodologies and analytical techniques to minimise their effects. Additionally, transparent reporting and peer review processes contribute to the overall robustness of medical research by scrutinising and validating study methods and results.

Chapter 5

Sampling Techniques and Sample Size Determination

Sampling techniques refer to the methods used by researchers to select a subset of individuals or elements from a larger population for the purpose of study. The goal is to obtain a representative sample that accurately reflects the characteristics of the entire population Sampling techniques play a crucial role in medical research, contributing significantly to the validity, reliability, and generalisability of study findings. The importance of employing appropriate sampling techniques in medical research is multifaceted and extends across various aspects of study design, data collection, and the interpretation of results.

Understanding the terminology associated with sampling techniques is crucial for researchers to design and conduct studies effectively. Here are key terms commonly used in the context of sampling techniques:

- **Population:** The entire group of individuals, cases, or elements that meet the criteria for inclusion in a study. The population is the target group from which a sample is drawn.
- **Sample:** A subset of the population selected for study. The characteristics and behaviours of the sample are used to make inferences about the larger population.
- **Sampling Frame:** A list or representation of the elements in the population from which the sample is drawn. It serves as a practical basis for selecting participants.
- **Sampling Unit:** The individual elements or units included in the sampling frame. For example, individuals, households, or specific time intervals may serve as sampling units.

- **Sampling Technique:** The procedure used to select individuals or elements from the population to be included in the sample. Common techniques include random sampling, stratified sampling, and convenience sampling.

There are two main types of sampling techniques: **probability sampling** and **non-probability sampling**. Probability sampling involves random selection, allowing you to make strong statistical inferences about the whole group. Non-probability sampling involves non-random selection based on convenience or other criteria, allowing you to easily collect data.

The table summarises some of the common sampling techniques and their subtypes, along with their advantages and disadvantages.

Sampling Technique	Subtype	Description	Advantages	Disadvantages
Probability Sampling	Simple Random Sampling	Every member of the population has an equal chance of being selected for the sample.	Representative, unbiased, easy to analyse.	Requires a complete list of the population, may not capture diversity or complexity.
	Simple Random Sampling	Every member of the population has an equal chance of being selected for the sample.	Representative, unbiased, easy to analyse.	Requires a complete list of the population, may not capture diversity or complexity.
	Systematic Sampling	Every nth member of the population is selected for the sample.	Representative, unbiased, easy to implement.	Requires a complete list of the population, may introduce periodicity or bias.

Sampling Technique	Subtype	Description	Advantages	Disadvantages
	Stratified Sampling	The population is divided into subgroups or strata based on certain characteristics, and then a random sample is taken from each stratum.	Representative, reduces sampling error, ensures proportional representation.	Requires prior knowledge of the population, may increase complexity or cost.
	Cluster Sampling	The population is divided into clusters or groups, and then a random sample of clusters is selected. Then, all members of the selected clusters are included in the sample.	Reduces cost and logistical difficulties, suitable for large or dispersed populations.	May introduce cluster bias, may reduce precision or accuracy.
	Multi-Stage Sampling	Combines two or more sampling techniques.	Allows flexibility and customisation, suitable for complex or heterogeneous populations.	May increase complexity or cost, may introduce multiple sources of error or bias.
Non-Probability sampling	Convenience Sampling	The sample is selected based on availability or accessibility.	Easy, fast, inexpensive, suitable for exploratory or pilot studies.	Unrepresentative, biased, unreliable, cannot generalize findings.

Sampling Technique	Subtype	Description	Advantages	Disadvantages
	Quota Sampling	The sample is selected to match the proportions of certain characteristics in the population.	Ensures representation of relevant groups, suitable for descriptive or comparative studies.	Unrepresentative, biased, unreliable, cannot generalize findings.
	Purposive Sampling	The sample is selected based on specific criteria or purpose.	Allows in-depth exploration of a phenomenon or group, suitable for qualitative or case studies.	Unrepresentative, biased, subjective, cannot generalize findings.
	Snowball Sampling	The sample is selected by asking existing participants to recruit more participants.	Allows access to hard-to-reach or hidden populations, suitable for sensitive or niche topics.	Unrepresentative, biased, dependent on initial participants, cannot generalize findings.

Practical applications of some sampling techniques in health research:

Simple random sampling:

Simple random sampling is important in health research to fairly choose participants. In a study on hypertension among 40 to 60-year-olds in a city, researchers pick people randomly by using a list and assigning numbers. They then use a method, like a number generator, to select a group (e.g., 100 people). This ensures everyone has an equal chance of being chosen. This helps researchers say things about the whole population accurately. The study gives insights into how many people in the city, aged 40 to 60, might have hypertension.

Systematic Sampling:

In health research, systematic sampling is a method where every nth individual is selected from a list after choosing a random starting point. For instance, consider a study on patient satisfaction in a hospital with a list of 500 patients. Using systematic sampling, researchers might select every 10th patient on the list, starting randomly. If the random starting point is the 3rd patient, the sample would include patients 3, 13, 23, and so on. This method is efficient when a systematic pattern is present, providing a representative sample and simplifying the selection process compared to random sampling. To determine the sampling interval in systematic sampling, first, identify the total population size (N) and the desired sample size (n). Calculate the sampling interval (k) using the formula = k = N/n, representing the number of elements between each selected individual. After selecting a random starting point, systematically choose every k^{th} element until the sample size is achieved, ensuring an efficient and representative sampling process.

Stratified Sampling

In health research, stratified sampling is a method used to ensure representation from different subgroups within a population. For instance, consider a study on the prevalence of diabetes in an urban community with diverse socioeconomic backgrounds. To implement stratified sampling, researchers first identify relevant strata, such as income levels. Subsequently, they randomly select individuals from each stratum, ensuring proportional representation. For example, if there are three income strata (low, medium, high), the researchers might select 20 individuals from each, resulting in a more comprehensive and balanced sample. Stratified sampling enables researchers to capture variations within specific subgroups, providing a more nuanced understanding of health outcomes in diverse socioeconomic contexts.

Cluster Sampling

In health research, cluster sampling is a method where the population is divided into clusters, and entire clusters are randomly selected for inclusion in the study. For instance, consider a study on vaccination coverage in rural communities. The clusters could be villages, and researchers might randomly select a few villages for the study. Within the chosen villages, all eligible individuals would be included in the sample. This approach simplifies data collection, especially when the population is dispersed, and can be more cost-effective. However, it requires accounting for potential intra-cluster similarities, as individuals within the same cluster may share common characteristics. Cluster sampling is particularly useful in studies where the population is naturally organized into groups, making it impractical to sample individuals separately.

Sample size calculations.

Sample size considerations are crucial in medical research as they directly impact the validity, reliability, and generalisability of study findings. Determining an appropriate sample size involves careful consideration of several factors:

- **Study Objectives**: Clearly define the research objectives and the specific outcomes or effects your aim to detect. The complexity and magnitude of these objectives influence the required sample size.
- **Effect Size**: The effect size represents the magnitude of the difference or association being investigated. A larger effect size generally requires a smaller sample size to achieve statistical significance.
- **Statistical Power**: Statistical power is the probability of detecting a true effect if it exists. Researchers typically aim for a power of 80% or higher. Higher power often necessitates a larger sample size.
- **Significance Level (Alpha)**: The significance level (alpha) is the probability of rejecting a true null hypothesis. Commonly set at 0.05, a lower alpha level increases the probability of Type II errors but may require a larger sample size.
- **Population Variability**: The variability within the population, often represented by the standard deviation, influences sample size

calculations. Greater variability usually requires a larger sample size to achieve precision.

- **Confidence Interval Width**: The desired width of the confidence interval around the estimated effect size affects the sample size. A narrower interval, reflecting greater precision, may require a larger sample.
- **Study Design**: The study design, such as cross-sectional, cohort, or clinical trial, influences the sample size calculation. Complex designs or those with multiple comparisons may require larger samples.
- **Type of Analysis**: The statistical analysis method, whether parametric or non-parametric, and the complexity of the analysis plan impact sample size considerations.
- **Practical Constraints**: Consider logistical constraints, budget limitations, and ethical considerations when determining the feasible sample size. Striking a balance between scientific rigor and practical feasibility is essential.
- **Expected Attrition**: Account for potential participant dropout or loss to follow-up. Adjust the initial sample size to accommodate expected attrition and maintain statistical power.
- **Context of Previous Research:** Reviewing similar studies or existing literature can provide insights into expected effect sizes and population variability, guiding the determination of an appropriate sample size.

Conducting a sample size calculation early in the research planning phase is essential for designing studies with sufficient power to detect meaningful effects. It contributes to the overall robustness and reliability of medical research findings, ensuring that results are both statistically and clinically significant.

Sample size calculation for descriptive study.

Calculating the sample size for a descriptive study involves determining the number of participants needed to adequately describe the characteristics of a population. The sample size depends on factors such as the desired level of precision, the variability in the population, and the chosen confidence level. To determine the sample size for a descriptive study, first, clearly identify the specific features you want to study within the population. Next, decide on the maximum acceptable difference between the sample estimate and the actual population value – this is the margin of error. Choose a confidence level, like 95% or 99%, indicating the likelihood that the true population value falls within the calculated range. If possible, estimate the variability (standard deviation) within the population; if not, use a standard deviation from a similar study or make a conservative estimate.

For qualitative variable

$$\text{Sample size} = \frac{Z_{1-\alpha/2}^{2}\,SD^{2}}{d^{2}}$$

$Z_{1-\alpha/2}$ = Is standard normal variate (at 5% type 1 error ($P<0.05$) it is 1.96 and at 1% type 1 error ($P<0.01$) it is 2.58). As in majority of studies P values are considered significant below 0.05 hence 1.96 is used in formula.

p = Expected proportion in population based on previous studies or pilot studies.

d = Absolute error or precision – Has to be decided by researcher.

For quantitative variable

$$\text{Sample size} = \frac{Z_{1-\alpha/2}^{2}\,p(1-p)}{d^{2}}$$

$Z_{1-\alpha/2}$ = Is standard normal variate as mentioned in previous section.

SD = Standard deviation of variable. Value of standard deviation can be taken from previously done study or through pilot study.

d = Absolute error or precision as mentioned in previous section

Sample size calculation for case control studies.

Calculating sample size for a case-control study involves defining parameters, including prevalence in controls, significance level, and desired power. Estimating the effect size, typically represented as odds ratio, helps determine the required sample size using a formula. Adjustments for non-response or loss to follow-up are essential considerations. Utilizing statistical software or tables streamlines the calculation process, ensuring the study is adequately powered for reliable results.

For qualitative variable

$$\text{Sample size} = \frac{r+1}{r} \frac{(p^*)(1-p^*)(Z_\beta + Z_{\alpha/2})^2}{(p_1 - p_2)^2}$$

r = Ratio of control to cases, 1 for equal number of case and control

p^* = Average proportion exposed = proportion of exposed cases + proportion of control exposed/2

Z_β = Standard normal variate for power = for 80% power it is 0.84 and for 90% value is 1.28. Researcher has to select power for the study.

$Z_{\alpha/2}$ = Standard normal variate for level of significance as mentioned in previous section.

$p_1 - p_2$ = Effect size or different in proportion expected based on previous studies. p_1 is proportion in cases and p_2 is proportion in control.

For quantitative variable

$$\text{Sample size} = \frac{r+1}{r} \frac{SD^2(Z_\beta + Z_{\alpha/2})^2}{d^2}$$

SD = Standard deviation = researcher can take value from previously published studies

d = Expected mean difference between case and control (may be based on previously published studies.)

r, Z_β, $Z_{\alpha/2}$ are already explained in previous sections.

Sample size calculation of cohort studies.

Calculating sample size for cohort studies involves defining key parameters like expected outcome incidence, significance level, and desired power.

$$\text{Sample size} = \frac{\left[Z_\alpha \sqrt{\left(1+\frac{1}{m}\right)p^*(1-p^*)} + Z_\beta \sqrt{p1} \atop (1-p1)/m + p2(1-p2)\right]^2}{(p_1 - p_2)^2}$$

Z_α = Standard normal variate for level of significance

m = Number of control subject per experimental subject

Z_β = Standard normal variate for power or type 2 error as explained in earlier section

$p1$ = Probability of events in control group

$p2$ = Probability of events in experimental group p

$$P^* = \frac{p2 + m\,p1}{m+1}$$

Sample size calculation for Clinical trials or clinical interventional studies.

Calculating sample size for clinical trials involves defining parameters like the expected treatment effect, variability in outcomes, and significance levels. In the context of comparing two groups and assessing quantitative data like blood sugar or haemoglobin level, the sample size can be determined using the subsequent formula.

$$\text{Sample size} = \frac{2SD^2(Z_{\alpha/2} + Z_\beta)^2}{d^2}$$

SD – Standard deviation = From previous studies or pilot study

$Z_{\alpha/2} = Z_{0.05/2} = Z_{0.025} = 1.96$ (From Z table) at type 1 error of 5%

$Z_\beta = Z_{0.20} = 0.842$ (From Z table) at 80% power

d = effect size = difference between mean values

If a clinical intervention study focuses on qualitative endpoints such as mortality or morbidity status, the sample size for comparing two groups can be calculated using the following formula.

$$\text{Sample size} = \frac{2(Z_{\alpha/2} + Z_{\beta})^2\,P(1-P)}{(p_1 - p_2)^2}$$

$Z_{\alpha/2} = Z_{0.05/2} = Z_{0.025} = 1.96$ (From Z table) at type 1 error of 5%

$Z_{\beta} = Z_{0.20} = 0.842$ (From Z table) at 80% power

$p_1 - p_2$ = Difference in proportion of events in two groups

P = Pooled prevalence = [prevalence in case group (p_1) + prevalence in control group (p_2)]/2

Sample size calculations using G power.

G power is a free and user-friendly software that can help you calculate the sample size and power for various statistical tests, such as t-tests, ANOVA, correlation, and more. You can also use G power to perform post-hoc analysis and sensitivity analysis. To use G power, you need to follow these steps:

- Select the test family and the statistical test that match your research question. For example, if you want to compare the means of two independent groups, you can choose the t-test family and the Means: Difference between two independent means tests.
- Choose the type of power analysis you want to perform. There are five options:

    1. A priori (to compute sample size given power, alpha, and effect size).
    2. Post hoc (to compute achieved power given sample size, alpha, and effect size).
    3. Compromise (to compute a reasonable sample size given power, alpha, and a range of effect sizes). Criterion (to compute the minimum effect size that can be detected given power, alpha, and sample size).
    4. Sensitivity (to compute the range of effect sizes that can be detected given power, alpha, and sample size).

Enter the input parameters for your analysis, such as the effect size, the alpha level, the power level, and the sample size (depending on the type of analysis you chose). You can also adjust other options, such as the allocation ratio, the correlation, and the non-centrality parameter.

Click on the Calculate button to obtain the output of your analysis. You can also view the graphical display of your analysis by clicking on the Graph x or Graph y buttons.

Chapter 6

Inferential statistics

Inferential statistics is a branch of statistics that involves drawing conclusions or inferences about a population based on a sample of data from that population. It uses statistical methods to make predictions, estimate parameters, and test hypotheses about the characteristics of a larger group. Inferential statistics allows researchers to generalize findings from a subset of data to the broader population, providing insights into relationships, trends, or effects that may exist beyond the observed sample. Key terms commonly used in inferential statistics, to describe the processes and outcomes are:

- **Population:** The entire group that is the subject of the study or analysis.
- **Sample:** A subset of the population selected for the study, often used to make inferences about the entire population.
- **Parameter:** A numerical value that describes a characteristic of a population.
- **Statistic:** A numerical value that describes a characteristic of a sample.
- **Standard error:** It is a measure of the variability or precision of a sample statistic, indicating how much the sample mean or other estimate is likely to deviate from the true population parameter. The types of standard errors are.

  - **Standard Error of the Mean (SEM):** Measures the variability of sample means and is calculated as the standard deviation of the sample divided by the square root of the sample size.
  - **Standard Error of Regression (SER or SE):** Estimates the variability of the regression coefficients in linear regression

analysis, providing a measure of how much the estimated coefficients might differ from the true population values.

- o **Standard Error of Proportion**: Pertains to estimating the variability of sample proportions, commonly used in the context of estimating proportions or percentages in categorical data.

- **Statistical estimation:** It involves the process of estimating unknown parameters of a population based on sample data. The types of statistical estimation are.

  - o **Point Estimation**: It provides a single, specific value as an estimate for the unknown population parameter.
  - o **Interval Estimation**: It provides a range, or interval, within which the true value of the population parameter is likely to fall, along with a level of confidence.

- **Hypothesis Testing:** A statistical method used to make inferences about a population parameter based on sample data.
- **Null Hypothesis (H0):** A statement that there is no significant difference or effect, often the default assumption in hypothesis testing.
- **Alternative Hypothesis (H1):** A statement that contradicts the null hypothesis, suggesting a significant difference or effect.
- **Significance Level (α):** The probability of rejecting the null hypothesis when it is true, commonly set at 0.05.
- **P-Value:** The probability of obtaining results as extreme as those observed, assuming the null hypothesis is true; used to determine statistical significance.
- **Confidence Interval:** A range of values that likely contains the true population parameter, along with a level of confidence.
- **Sampling Distribution:** The distribution of a statistic, such as the mean or proportion, calculated from multiple samples of the same size taken from the population.
- **Degrees of freedom**: It represent the number of independent pieces of information utilized in computing a statistic and are determined by subtracting the number of restrictions from the sample size. For instance, when estimating the mean from a sample of 10 observations, there are 9 degrees of freedom as one observation is constrained by

the sample mean. Degrees of freedom play a crucial role in hypothesis testing, influencing the distribution of the test statistic. Various tests employ distinct formulas to calculate degrees of freedom, contingent upon the type and quantity of parameters involved. For instance, a t-test involves n – 1 degrees of freedom (where n is the sample size), while a chi-square test involves k – 1 degrees of freedom (where k is the number of categories).

- **Central Limit Theorem:** A fundamental principle stating that the distribution of the sample mean approaches a normal distribution as the sample size increases, regardless of the shape of the population distribution.
- **Power of a Test:** The probability of correctly rejecting a false null hypothesis (1 – Type II error).
- **One-tailed test** : It is a hypothesis test that specifies the direction of the effect, such as greater than or less than.
- **Two-tailed test**: It is a hypothesis test that does not specify the direction of the effect, but only that there is a difference.

For example, for testing whether a new drug lowers blood pressure, a one-tailed test with the alternative hypothesis that the drug reduces blood pressure can be employed. However, when testing whether a new drug affects blood pressure in any direction, a two-tailed test with the alternative hypothesis that the drug changes blood pressure is suitable. One-tailed tests offer the advantage of increased power to detect effects in the specified

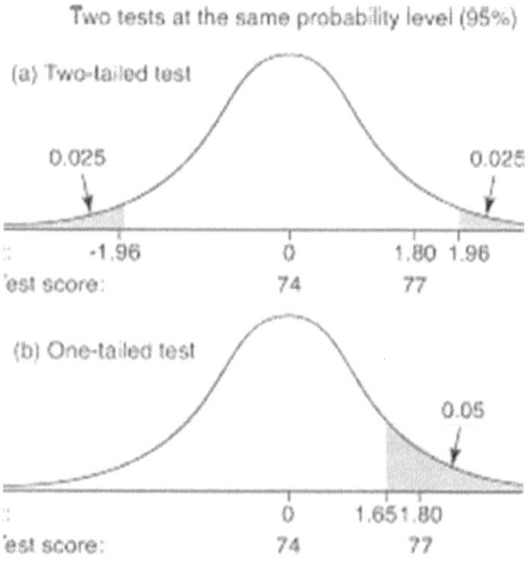

direction but have the disadvantage of potentially overlooking effects in the opposite direction. On the contrary, two-tailed tests are more conservative and less prone to false positives but require a larger effect size to reject the null hypothesis.

- **Effect size**: It is a measure of the magnitude or importance of the difference between two groups or the relationship between two variables. Effect size helps to determine the practical significance of a research finding, beyond the statistical significance. Effect size is independent of the sample size, unlike the p-value. Cohen's d is one of the most common ways to measure effect size for the difference between two means.

The formula for Cohen's d is.

$$D = \frac{M_1 - M_2}{S_p}$$

M1 and M2 represent the sample means for the two groups being compared and Sp represents the pooled estimated population standard deviation.

$$S_p = \sqrt{\frac{(N_1 - 1) \cdot S_1^2 + (N_2 - 1) \cdot S_2^2}{N_1 + N_2 - 2}}$$

N represents the mean for each group (as numbered), $S1^2$ and $S2^2$ represents the spread of values within each group.

The general guidelines for interpreting the effect size are as follows:

0.2 = small effect, 0.5 = moderate effect, 0.8 = large effect

Sampling error and Non – sampling error

Sampling error	Non-sampling error
A statistical error that occurs when the sample does not represent the entire population of interest.	An error that occurs due to sources other than sampling, such as human, procedural, or technical errors.
A random error that varies depending on the sample size and sampling method.	A systematic error that can be random or non-random and affects both sample and census.

Sampling error	Non-sampling error
Caused by the deviation between the sample mean and the population mean.	Caused by the deficiency and analysis of data, such as error in problem definition, questionnaire design, data collection, processing, or interpretation.
Can be reduced by increasing the sample size.	Has nothing to do with the sample size and can be reduced by improving the quality of data.

Hypothesis

A hypothesis is a tentative statement that can be tested and potentially proven or disproven through further investigation and experimentation. It is often used in scientific research to guide the design of experiments and the collection and analysis of data. A hypothesis is an assumption that is made based on some evidence and is used to test the relationship between two or more variables. There are different types of hypotheses, but the two major ones are:

- **Null hypothesis**: This type of hypothesis proposes no relationship between the variables. It is a negative statement that is often used to test the significance of the results. Example : 'Smoking has no effect on the risk of lung cancer'
- **Alternative hypothesis**: This type of hypothesis proposes a relationship between the variables. It is a positive statement that is often used to show the expected direction of the results. Example : 'Smoking increases the risk of lung cancer'.

Alpha error and beta error

Alpha error and beta error are two types of errors that can occur in statistical hypothesis testing. Alpha error, also known as Type I error, is the probability of rejecting a true null hypothesis. Beta error, also known as Type II error, is the probability of failing to reject a false null hypothesis.

Table that summarises the concepts of alpha error and beta error

Null hypothesis (H0)	True	False
Reject H0	Alpha error (false positive)	Correct decision (true negative)
Fail to reject H0	Correct decision (true positive)	Beta error (false negative)

In a study testing a new drug aim to lower blood pressure, if the researchers wrongly reject the idea that the drug has no effect (Type I error), they might incorrectly believe the drug is effective when it's not. This mistake could lead to approving a drug that might not actually work, posing risks to patients. On the other hand, if the drug does help lower blood pressure but the study fails to identify this effect (Type II error), the researchers might miss recognizing the drug's potential benefits, resulting in lost chances for better patient care.

One way to reduce alpha error is by opting for a smaller significance level in the hypothesis test, demanding stronger evidence against the null hypothesis for rejection. Nevertheless, this reduction in alpha error might elevate the risk of Type II error, and although increasing the sample size can help mitigate alpha error, practical constraints like cost and time may limit its feasibility, necessitating alternative statistical approaches or adjustments to research design.

To minimise beta error, consider augmenting the sample size, which decreases data variability and enhances the ability to identify a genuine effect. Alternatively, increasing the effect size, denoting a more prominent difference between groups or a stronger relationship between variables, can also mitigate beta error. Another approach is raising the significance level, indicating a greater willingness to reject the null hypothesis, even with a potential increase in the risk of Type I error.

Confidence interval

A confidence interval is a range of values that you expect your estimate to fall between a certain percentage of the time if you repeat your experiment or re-sample the population in the same way. The confidence level represents the frequency with which you anticipate replicating an estimate within the upper and lower limits of the confidence interval. This level is determined by the alpha value.

In a study examining how a new medicine lowers blood pressure, researchers find a 95% confidence interval for the average blood pressure reduction (e.g., 5 mmHg to 8 mmHg). This means that in many repetitions of the study, about 95% of the intervals calculated would capture the real average blood pressure reduction.

To break it down:

- The estimated middle point is 6.5 mmHg.
- The range (5 mmHg to 8 mmHg) is where we feel 95% confident the actual average blood pressure reduction is located.
- If the range doesn't include zero, it suggests a significant effect.

In simpler terms, the confidence interval helps researchers show how sure they are about their findings. In this blood pressure study, it indicates we're quite sure the true average reduction is in that range. A wider range means less certainty, while a narrower one means more confidence. Confidence intervals are useful for explaining how dependable and variable research results are in health studies.

Level of significance

The level of significance, denoted as α, is a pivotal concept in medical statistics, guiding the determination of statistical significance. Commonly set at 0.05, it signifies that results are deemed statistically significant if the likelihood of their occurrence due to random chance is less than 5%. This significance level plays a crucial role in various aspects of medical research and decision-making. In hypothesis testing, it informs the acceptance or rejection of null hypotheses, particularly in clinical trials where it influences the assessment of treatment efficacy. The level of significance also impacts the precision of confidence intervals, contributes to risk assessment in medical decisions, aids in meta-analysis by assigning weight to individual study findings, and informs the development of public health policies based on epidemiological associations. Adhering to a chosen level of significance ensures a rigorous and standardized approach to statistical interpretation in medical contexts.

Probability and the 'P value'

In statistics, probability is a measure that quantifies the likelihood of a particular event or outcome occurring. It is expressed as a number between 0 and 1, where 0 indicates impossibility and 1 indicates certainty. The probability of an event A is denoted as $P(A)$.

Probability theory is a fundamental concept in statistics, serving as the basis for inferential statistics, hypothesis testing, and Bayesian analysis, among other statistical methods. It allows researchers and analysts to make predictions and draw conclusions from data in the presence of uncertainty.

The p-value, or probability value, is a crucial statistical measure that quantifies the evidence against a null hypothesis. It represents the probability of obtaining observed results or more extreme results under the assumption that the null hypothesis is true. In other words, it assesses whether the observed data is consistent with what would be expected if there were no real effect or difference.

Significance of P Value:

- **Hypothesis Testing:** The p-value is central to hypothesis testing. A small p-value (typically ≤ 0.05) suggests strong evidence against the null hypothesis, leading to its rejection. Conversely, a larger p-value indicates weaker evidence, failing to reject the null hypothesis.
- **Statistical Significance:** A p-value below a chosen significance level (e.g., 0.05) is often interpreted as statistically significant. This suggests that the observed results are unlikely to have occurred by random chance alone, supporting the presence of a real effect or association.
- **Decision-Making in Research:** Researchers use p-values to make informed decisions about the significance of their findings. If the p-value is significant, it may influence the acceptance of a new hypothesis or the effectiveness of a treatment.

- **Confidence Intervals:** The p-value is closely linked to confidence intervals. A low p-value corresponds to a narrow confidence interval, indicating increased precision in estimating the true population parameter.
- **Risk Assessment:** In medical research, p-values are crucial for assessing the risk associated with certain outcomes or interventions. They help identify whether observed effects are likely due to the intervention or simply due to chance.
- **Publication Standards:** Journals and scientific publications often use p-values to determine whether study results meet the criteria for publication. Studies with statistically significant findings are more likely to be accepted for publication.
- **Interpretation of Study Findings:** The p-value aids in the interpretation of study findings by providing a quantitative measure of the strength of evidence against the null hypothesis. It assists in distinguishing between random variation and true effects.

Key Points:

- Smaller p-values signify stronger evidence against the null hypothesis.
- Larger p-values suggest weaker evidence against the null hypothesis.

In statistical terms, researchers often use a significance level (commonly 0.05) as a threshold, considering p-values below this level as grounds for rejecting the null hypothesis and accepting the presence of a statistically significant effect. A finding can be statistically significant but not clinically meaningful, and vice versa. Researchers and practitioners should consider both statistical and clinical significance when interpreting study results, ensuring that observed effects are not only reliable but also relevant in practical settings.

Hypothesis testing

Hypothesis testing is a statistical method that is used to decide about a claim, or a prediction based on data. It involves the following steps:

- Formulate a null hypothesis (H0) and an alternative hypothesis (H1) that are mutually exclusive and exhaustive. The null hypothesis is usually a statement of no effect or no difference, while the alternative hypothesis is the opposite or the one that you want to support.

- Choose a significance level (alpha), which is the probability of rejecting the null hypothesis when it is true. A common choice is 0.05 or 5%.
- Calculate a test statistic using the data and the hypotheses. The test statistic measures how far the data are from the null hypothesis.
- To assess the null hypothesis, compare the test statistic to the critical value or p-value. If the test statistic exceeds the critical value or the p-value is below the significance level, reject the null hypothesis; otherwise, fail to reject it and do not accept the alternative hypothesis. Report and interpret the results of the hypothesis test in the context of the research question.

Hypothesis testing is a useful tool for making inferences about a population based on a sample. However, it has some limitations and assumptions that need to be considered, such as the type and size of the sample, the distribution and variability of the data, and the possibility of type I and type II errors.

Chapter 7

Test of Significance

A test of significance is a statistical method that helps to determine whether the results of study are likely to be due to chance or not. It involves comparing the observed data with a claim or a hypothesis about a population parameter, such as the mean or the proportion.

The key steps in a typical test of significance:

1. **Formulate hypotheses:** Establish a null hypothesis (often denoted as H0) representing a default or no-effect assumption, and an alternative hypothesis (often denoted as H1) suggesting a specific effect or difference.
2. **Choose significance level (α):** Select a significance level, denoted as α, which represents the probability of making a Type I error (rejecting a true null hypothesis). Common choices include 0.05, 0.01, or 0.10.
3. **Collect and analyse data:** Gather data through experiments, surveys, or observations. Use appropriate statistical tests to analyse the data and calculate a test statistic.
4. **Determine critical region:** Define a critical region or rejection region based on the chosen significance level. If the test statistic falls within this region, the null hypothesis is rejected.
5. **Calculate P-value:** Compute the p-value, which represents the probability of obtaining results as extreme as the observed data, assuming the null hypothesis is true.
6. **Compare P-value to α:** If the p-value is less than or equal to the significance level (α), reject the null hypothesis. Otherwise, fail to reject the null hypothesis.
7. **Draw conclusions:** Conclude whether the results provide sufficient evidence to reject the null hypothesis in favour of the alternative hypothesis.

Tests of significance can be broadly classified into two categories:

- **Parametric tests**
- **Non-parametric tests.**

Parameter	Parametric Test	Nonparametric Test
Assumptions	Assume normal distribution and equal variance of the data	Do not assume any specific distribution or variance of the data
Data type	Require interval or ratio data	Can handle nominal or ordinal data
Robustness	Sensitive to outliers and violations of assumptions	More robust to outliers and violations of assumptions
Power	More powerful and precise when assumptions are met	Less powerful and precise when assumptions are not met
Examples	t-test, ANOVA, Pearson's correlation	Sign test, Wilcoxon test, Kruskal-Wallis test, Spearman's correlation

Common parametric and nonparametric tests and their purpose

Parametric Test	Nonparametric Test	Purpose
t-test	Mann-Whitney U test	Compare the means or medians of two independent groups.
ANOVA	Kruskal-Wallis test	Compare the means or medians of more than two independent groups.
Paired t-test	Wilcoxon signed-rank test	Compare the means or medians of two paired or matched groups.
Pearson's correlation	Spearman's correlation	Measure the linear or monotonic relationship between two variables.
	Chi-square test	Assesses whether there is a significant association between categorical variables by comparing observed and expected frequencies.

Correlation: It is a statistical technique used to measure the strength and direction of the linear relationship between two quantitative variables. It provides a numerical value, known as the correlation coefficient, which quantifies how well the movements of one variable predict the movements of another.

Regression: Regression analysis is a statistical technique used to model the relationship between a dependent variable and one or more independent variables. The primary goal of regression is to understand and quantify the impact of changes in the independent variables on the dependent variable. It helps in making predictions or estimates based on the observed data.

Correlation	Regression
Measures the strength and direction of the linear association between two variables.	Measures the effect of one variable (predictor) on another variable (response).
Both variables are treated equally, without distinction between dependent and independent.	Variables are distinguished as dependent (response) and independent (predictor).
The main goal is to quantify the degree of correlation between the variables.	The main goal is to estimate the value of the response variable based on the value of the predictor variable.
The correlation coefficient ® ranges from – 1 to 1, indicating the direction and magnitude of the correlation.	The regression coefficient (b) indicates the average change in the response variable for a unit change in the predictor variable.

Tests of significances related to comparison of means.

Parametric tests

Unpaired or Independent sample t test:

The Unpaired or Independent Sample t-test is a statistical test used to compare the means of two independent groups to determine if there is a significant difference between them. It is commonly employed when the data from two groups are independent of each other, meaning that the observations in one group are unrelated to the observations in the other. Unpaired t test is used to compare the mean outcomes between two independent groups, such as those receiving different treatments in a clinical trial.

Assumptions:

- The observations in one sample are independent of the observations in the other sample.
- The data in both samples are approximately normally distributed.
- The variances of both samples are roughly equal.
- The data in both samples were obtained using a random sampling method.

Steps:

1. Define the null and alternative hypotheses. The null hypothesis states that there is no significant difference between the means of the two groups. The alternative hypothesis states that there is a significant difference between the means of the two groups, either in a specific direction (one-tailed test) or in any direction (two-tailed test).
2. Choose a significance level (alpha). This is the probability of rejecting the null hypothesis when it is true. A common choice is 0.05, which means that there is a 5% chance of making a type I error (false positive).
3. Calculate the test statistic (t).

   The t-test equation for when samples have equal variances is:

   $$t = \frac{(\bar{x}_1 - \bar{x}_2)}{s_p \sqrt{1/n_1 + 1/n_2}}$$

   $\bar{x}_1$ where is the mean of the first sample, $\bar{x}_2$ is the mean of the second sample, s_p is the pooled standard deviation, n_1 is the sample size of the first sample, and n_2 is the sample size of the second sample.

   The t-test equation for when samples do not have equal variances is:

   $$t = \frac{(\bar{x}_1 - \bar{x}_2)}{\sqrt{\frac{s_1^2}{n_1} + \frac{s_2^2}{n_2}}}$$

$\bar{x}_1$ where is the mean of the first sample, $\bar{x}_2$ is the mean of the second sample, s_1 is the standard deviation of first sample and s_2 is the standard deviation of second sample, n_1 is the sample size of the first sample, and n_2 is the sample size of the second sample.

4. Find the critical value (t^*) and the p-value. The critical value is the value of t that corresponds to the chosen significance level and the degrees of freedom of the test. The degrees of freedom depend on the sample sizes and whether the variances of the two groups are assumed to be equal or not. The p-value is the probability of obtaining a test statistic as extreme or more extreme than the observed one, under the null hypothesis. The p-value can be found using a t-distribution table or a calculator.

5. Compare the test statistic with the critical value or the p-value with the significance level and decide. If the test statistic is more extreme than the critical value, or the p-value is less than the significance level, then reject the null hypothesis and conclude that there is a significant difference between the means of the two groups. Otherwise, fail to reject the null hypothesis and conclude that there is no significant difference between the means of the two groups.

Paired t-test:

A paired t-test is a statistical test that compares the means of two samples that are related or matched in some way, such as before and after measurements, or observations from the same individuals. Paired t-test is used to evaluate the impact of an intervention (such as a medication, therapy, or lifestyle change) on health outcomes by comparing measurements before and after the intervention.

Assumptions:

- The dependent variable is continuous (interval or ratio).
- The observations are independent of each other.
- The differences between the pairs are approximately normally distributed.
- There are no extreme outliers in the differences.

Steps:

1. Subtract each value in the second sample from the corresponding value in the first sample. This will give you the differences between the pairs.
2. Calculate the mean and the standard deviation of the differences.
3. Calculate the test statistic using the formula.

$$t = \frac{\sum d}{\sqrt{\frac{n(\sum d^2) - (\sum d)^2}{n-1}}}$$

Where, $\sum d$ is the sum of the differences.

4. Find the critical value or the p-value for the t-statistic. You can use a t-table or a calculator to find the critical value or the p-value based on the degrees of freedom (n−1n−1) and the type of alternative hypothesis (two-sided or one-sided). The critical value is the value of t that corresponds to the significance level. The p-value is the probability of obtaining a t-statistic as extreme or more extreme than the observed one, assuming the null hypothesis is true.
5. Compare the t-statistic with the critical value or compare the p-value with the significance level, to decide about the null hypothesis. If the t-statistic is more extreme than the critical value, or if the p-value is less than the significance level, then you can reject the null hypothesis and conclude that there is a significant difference between the means of the two samples. Otherwise, you cannot reject the null hypothesis and conclude that there is no significant difference between the means of the two samples.

ANOVA (Analysis of Variance)

Analysis of Variance is a statistical method to compare the means of two or more groups. ANOVA can also help identify which groups are different from each other and by how much. ANOVA is based on the idea that the variability in the data can be partitioned into two sources: between-group variability and within-group variability.

There are different types of ANOVA depending on the number and nature of the independent variables, the number and nature of the dependent variables, and the design of the experiment or study.

The common types of ANOVA and their practical applications in health research are –

- **One-way ANOVA**: This is used when you have one independent variable with two or more levels, and one dependent variable. For example, you can use a one-way ANOVA to compare the mean blood pressure of patients who received different doses of a drug.
- **Two-way ANOVA**: This is used when you have two independent variables, each with two or more levels, and one dependent variable. For example, you can use a two-way ANOVA to compare the mean weight loss of participants who followed different diets and exercise regimes.
- **Repeated measures ANOVA**: This is used when you have one or more independent variables, and one dependent variable that is measured repeatedly over time or under different conditions. For example, you can use a repeated measures ANOVA to compare the mean pain scores of patients who underwent different surgical procedures at different time points.
- **MANOVA**: This stands for Multivariate Analysis of Variance, and it is used when you have one or more independent variables, and two or more dependent variables. For example, you can use a MANOVA to compare the mean scores of patients on different psychological tests after receiving different types of therapy.
- **ANCOVA**: This stands for Analysis of Covariance, and it is used when you have one or more independent variables, one dependent variable, and one or more covariates. Covariates are variables that are not of interest but may affect the outcome. For example, you can use an ANCOVA to compare the mean cholesterol levels of patients who received different treatments, while controlling for their age and gender.

Assumptions:

- The observations are independent of each other.
- The response variable follows a normal distribution in each group.
- The variances of the response variable are equal across the groups.

Steps:

1. Calculate the mean for each group.
2. Calculate the total mean. This is done by adding all the means and dividing it by the total number of means.
3. Calculate the SSB (Sum of squares between groups).
4. Calculate the between groups degrees of freedom.
5. Calculate the SSE (Sum of squares of errors).
6. Calculate the degrees of freedom of errors.
7. Determine the MSB (Mean squares between groups) and the MSE (Mean squares of errors).
8. Find the f test statistic.
9. Using the f table for the specified level of significance, α, find the critical value. This is given by F(α, df1. df2).
10. If f > F then reject the null hypothesis.

Non-Parametric tests

Mann – Whitney U test

The Mann-Whitney U test is a nonparametric statistical test that compares the ranks of two independent samples. It is used when the data are not normally distributed, and the sample sizes are small. The test can determine if there is a significant difference between the medians of the two groups. The Mann-Whitney U test is used to compare the effects of two different treatments, interventions, or exposures on a health-related outcome, such as blood pressure, pain level, quality of life, etc. The Mann-Whitney U test can also be used to compare the distributions of a health-related variable across two populations, such as patients and controls, males and females, smokers and non-smokers, etc.

Assumptions:

- The variable of interest is ordinal or continuous.
- The observations in each group are independent of each other and of the other group.
- The shape of the distributions for both groups is similar.

Steps:

1. State the null and alternative hypotheses. The null hypothesis is that the two populations are equal, and the alternative hypothesis is that they are not.
2. Choose a significance level, such as 0.05 or 0.01.
3. Calculate the test statistic U., which is the smaller of U_1 and U_2, where U_1 and U_2 are defined as

$$U_1 = n_1 n_2 + \frac{n_1(n_1 + 1)}{2} - R_1$$

$$U_2 = n_1 n_2 + \frac{n_2(n_2 + 1)}{2} - R_2$$

4. Here, n_1 and n_2 are the sample sizes for the two groups, and R_1 and R_2 are the sum of the ranks for the two groups.
5. Compare the test statistic with the critical value from the Mann-Whitney U table, based on the significance level and the degrees of freedom, which is the product of the sample sizes.
6. Reject or fail to reject the null hypothesis and interpret the results in the context of the research question.

Wilcoxon signed rank test.

The Wilcoxon signed-rank test is a nonparametric test that can compare the median of a single sample to a reference value, or the median difference between two paired samples. It is often used when the data are not normally distributed or have outliers. The Wilcoxon matched pairs signed rank test can be used to compare two different methods or interventions that measure the same variable on the same subjects. For example, when a health researcher might want to compare the accuracy and reliability of two different blood glucose meters by testing them on the same group of diabetic patients.

Assumptions:

- The paired samples or the single sample are random and independent.
- The measurement scale is at least ordinal, meaning that the values can be ranked in order.

- The variable under study is continuous or has many distinct values.
- The distribution of the differences between the paired values or the single values and the reference value is symmetric around zero.

Steps:

- State the null and alternative hypotheses. The null hypothesis is that the median difference between the two groups or the single group and the reference value is zero. The alternative hypothesis is that the median difference is not zero or has a specific direction (positive or negative).
- Find the difference and absolute difference for each pair or each value and the reference value. Ignore pairs or values that have a difference of zero, as they do not contribute to the test statistic.
- Order the pairs or values by the absolute differences and assign a rank from the smallest to largest absolute differences. If there are ties, assign the mean rank to the tied values.
- Find the sum of the positive ranks and the negative ranks. The positive ranks are the ranks of the pairs or values that have a positive difference, and the negative ranks are the ranks of the pairs or values that have a negative difference.
- Reject or fail to reject the null hypothesis. The test statistic, W, is the smaller of the absolute values of the positive ranks and negative ranks. To determine if we should reject or fail to reject the null hypothesis, we can compare W to a critical value from a table that corresponds to the sample size and the significance level. If W is less than or equal to the critical value, we can reject the null hypothesis. Otherwise, we fail to reject the null hypothesis.

Kruskal-Wallis test

The Kruskal-Wallis H test is a nonparametric statistical method that can be used to compare the medians of three or more independent groups. It is similar to the one-way ANOVA, but it does not require the assumption of normality or equal variances. It is based on the ranks of the data values rather than the actual data points. Kruskal-Wallis test can be used to compare the effectiveness of four different treatments for a disease condition.

Assumptions:

- The observations in each group are independent and random.
- The dependent variable is ordinal or continuous.
- The distributions of the groups have similar shapes.

Steps:

1. Rank all the data values from all groups together, from smallest to largest. Assign the average rank in case of ties.
2. Calculate the sum of the ranks for each group.
3. Use the rank sums to calculate the test statistic H using the formula:

$$H = \frac{12}{N(N+1)} \sum_{i=1}^{k} \frac{R_i^2}{n_i} - 3(N+1)$$

4. where N is the total number of observations, k is the number of groups, Ri is the sum of ranks for group i, and ni is the number of observations in group i.
5. Compare the value of H to the chi-square distribution with k–1 degrees of freedom. If H is greater than the critical value, reject the null hypothesis that the medians of the groups are equal.

Tests of significances related to comparison of proportions.

Chi – Square test(X2) :

Chi-square test is a statistical method used to test whether there is a significant difference or association between two or more categorical variables. Categorical variables are those that can only take a few specific values, such as gender, colour, or species. A chi-square test compares the observed frequencies of the variables to the expected frequencies under the null hypothesis, which is the assumption that there is no relationship between the variables.

Characteristics of chi-square test:

- They are non-parametric tests, meaning they do not require any assumptions about the distribution of the data.

- They can be used for both goodness of fit tests and tests of independence.
- They use a chi-square distribution, which is a skewed distribution that depends on the degrees of freedom, which is the number of categories minus one.
- They produce a p-value, which is the probability of obtaining a chi-square statistic as extreme or more extreme than the observed one, assuming the null hypothesis is true. A low p-value indicates that the null hypothesis can be rejected.

Practical applications of chi-square tests:

- To test the variance of a normal population.
- To test the independence of two categorical variables.
- To test the goodness of fit of a distribution.

Assumptions of chi-square tests:

- The data are randomly sampled from the population of interest.
- The variables are independent of each other, meaning that the value of one variable does not affect the value of another variable.
- The expected frequencies of each category are at least 5, or the chi-square test is adjusted using a correction factor such as Yates' correction or Fisher's exact test.

Steps:

1. Define the null and alternative hypotheses. The null hypothesis is usually that there is no difference or association between the variables, while the alternative hypothesis is that there is a difference or association.
2. Create a table of the observed and expected frequencies. The observed frequencies are the actual counts or proportions of the data, while the expected frequencies are the theoretical counts or proportions under the null hypothesis. A contingency table is a type of frequency distribution table that shows the number of observations in each combination of groups for two or more categorical variables.

3. Calculate the chi-square statistic using the formula.

$$x_c^2 = \frac{\Sigma\,(O_i - E_i)^2}{E_i}$$

c = Degrees of freedom, O = Observed Value, E = Expected Value

4. Find the degrees of freedom and the p-value. The degrees of freedom depend on the number of categories and the type of chi-square test. The p-value is the probability of obtaining a chi-square statistic as extreme or more extreme than the observed one, assuming the null hypothesis is true. You can use a table or a software to find the p-value based on the chi-square value and the degrees of freedom.

5. Compare the p-value to a significance level, usually 0.05. If the p-value is less than or equal to the significance level, you can reject the null hypothesis and conclude that there is a significant difference or association between the variables. If the p-value is greater than the significance level, you cannot reject the null hypothesis and conclude that there is no evidence of a difference or association.

Variants of chi-square test:

There are several variants of the chi-square test, each designed to address specific types of data or research questions. Some common variants include:

1. **Chi-square Test for Independence (or Association)**: This is the most common form of the test, used to determine whether there is a significant association between two categorical variables.

2. **Chi-square Test for Homogeneity**: Similar to the test for independence, this variant compares the distribution of one categorical variable across different groups of another categorical variable. It is often used when dealing with multiple independent groups.

3. **Chi-square Goodness-of-Fit Test**: This variant is employed when you want to assess whether the observed categorical data follows a specific expected distribution. It is commonly used in situations

where you want to compare observed and expected frequencies in a single categorical variable.

4. **Yates' Continuity Correction**: A modification applied to the basic chi-square test for 2x2 contingency tables, used to correct for potential inaccuracies when dealing with small sample sizes.

5. **Fisher's Exact Test**: A precise test used for 2x2 contingency tables when the chi-square test assumptions are not met or when dealing with small sample sizes. It provides an exact p-value without relying on the chi-square distribution.

6. **Mantel-Haenszel Test**: Used in the analysis of stratified 2x2 contingency tables, considering whether there is an association between two variables after controlling for the effects of a third variable (stratum).

7. **McNemar's test**: It is a statistical test for paired nominal data. It is used to compare the proportions of two related groups, such as before and after treatments, or matched pairs of subjects. The test is based on a 2x2 contingency table that shows the number of discordant pairs, where the two groups have different outcomes. The test statistic has a chi-squared distribution with one degree of freedom, and the p-value indicates the probability of observing the same or more extreme difference in proportions under the null hypothesis of no association.

Z test for proportions:

It is a statistical test that compares the proportions of two populations or groups when the population variance is known. It is used to test whether there is a significant difference or association between the proportions. Z test for proportion can be used in health research to test hypotheses about the prevalence of diseases, the effectiveness of treatments, the satisfaction of patients, and other topics involving proportions.

The pooled approach estimates the population proportion under the assumption of equal variances in the two samples. Conversely, the unpooled approach for the Z-test for proportions is similar to the pooled method but doesn't assume equal population proportions. Consequently, it calculates the standard error of the difference using individual sample proportions and their variances.

The formula for calculating the test statistic using the pooled approach:

$$z = \frac{(p_1 - p_2)}{\sqrt{\dfrac{p_{pooled}(1-p_{pooled})}{n_1} + \dfrac{p_{pooled}(1-p_{pooled})}{n_2}}}$$

$$p_{pooled} = \frac{p1 \cdot n1 + p2 \cdot n2}{n1 + n2}$$

p1: proportion of the first sample, p2: proportion of the second sample
n1: the size of the first sample, n2: the size of the second sample
p_pooled: pooled proportion

The formula for calculating the test statistic using the unpooled approach:

$$z = \frac{(p1 - p2)}{\sqrt{\dfrac{p1(1-p1)}{n1} + \dfrac{p2(1-p2)}{n2}}}$$

p1: proportion of the first sample, p2: proportion of the second sample
n1: the size of the first sample, n2: the size of the second sample

Chapter 8

Correlation

Correlation refers to the degree of association or relationship between two variables. It measures the extent to which changes in one variable are accompanied by changes in another variable. Correlation does not imply causation; it only indicates that there is a statistical relationship between the variables.

Correlation coefficient is a numerical measure of the strength and direction of the relationship between two variables.

Correlation analysis is essential in medical research for identifying relationships between variables, predicting outcomes, and assessing risks. It guides clinical decision-making by evaluating associations between symptoms, diagnostic tests, and treatment outcomes. Additionally, correlations inform quality improvement efforts and aid in designing effective research studies.

Assumptions

- **Linear relationship**: The variables should have a linear relationship, meaning that they change together at a constant rate.
- **Normality**: The variables should be normally distributed, meaning that they have a bell-shaped histogram or a Q-Q plot that follows a diagonal line.
- **No outliers**: The variables should not have any extreme values that deviate from the rest of the data.
- **No multicollinearity**: The variables should not be highly correlated with other variables in the analysis.

Types of Correlations

1. **Pearson's r**: This is the most widely used correlation coefficient for interval or ratio level variables. It measures the degree of linear association between two variables. Pearson's r is a valuable statistic in medical research, measuring the strength and direction of linear relationships between health-related variables like blood pressure and cholesterol. It aids researchers in exploring associations, testing hypotheses, and identifying potential confounding factors. However, its limitations, including sensitivity to outliers and inability to capture nonlinear relationships, underscore the importance of using Pearson's r cautiously along with other statistical methods, such as regression analysis, for drawing valid conclusions from medical data.

2. **Spearman's rho**: This is a non-parametric correlation coefficient for ordinal or ranked variables. It measures the degree of monotonic association between two variables, meaning that the variables tend to change together in the same or opposite direction, but not necessarily at a constant rate. It also ranges from –1 to +1, and it does not assume any distribution or linearity. Scatter plot with a smooth curve can be used to visualize the Spearman correlation between two variables. Despite its utility, Spearman's rho has limitations. It solely measures monotonic relationships, potentially missing nonlinear associations like U-shaped or S-shaped curves. Although less sensitive to outliers than Pearson's r, extreme values can still impact Spearman's rho. It's crucial to note that Spearman's rho does not imply causation, necessitating cautious use and supplementation with other statistical methods like regression analysis for drawing valid and meaningful conclusions in medical research.

3. **Kendall's tau**: This is another non-parametric correlation coefficient for ordinal or ranked variables. It measures the degree of concordance between two variables, meaning that the variables tend to have the same or different order of ranks. It ranges from –1 (perfect discordance) to +1 (perfect concordance), and it is less sensitive to outliers than Spearman's rho. You can use a scatter plot with a smooth curve to visualize the Kendall correlation between two variables.

4. **Point-Biserial correlation**: This is a special case of Pearson's r for dichotomous and continuous variables. It measures the degree of linear association between a binary variable (such as gender or presence/absence) and a continuous variable (such as height or weight). It also ranges from – 1 to +1, and it assumes that the continuous variable is normally distributed within each group of the binary variable. You can use a box plot or a histogram to visualize the Point-Biserial correlation between two variables.

Steps to calculate Pearson's correlation coefficient:

1. Calculate the mean of both variables by adding up all the values and dividing by the number of observations.
2. Calculate the difference between each value and the mean of its variable.
3. Calculate the product of the differences for each pair of values.
4. Sum up all the products from step 3. This is the numerator of the correlation coefficient formula.
5. Square each difference from step 2 and sum them up separately for each variable. This is the denominator of the correlation coefficient formula.
6. Take the square root of each sum from step 5 and multiply them together.
7. Divide the numerator by the denominator to get the correlation coefficient.

The formula for the correlation coefficient is:

$$r = \frac{n(\sum xy) - (\sum x)(\sum y)}{[n \sum x^2 - (\sum x)^2][n \sum y^2 - (\sum y)^2]}$$

n = Number of values or elements

$\sum$x = Sum of 1st values list

$\sum$y = Sum of 2nd values list

$\sum$xy = Sum of the product of 1st and 2nd values

$\sum$x2 = Sum of squares of 1st values

$\sum$y2 = Sum of squares of 2nd values

Interpretation of Correlation coefficient

Absolute Value of r	Strength of Correlation	Interpretation
0.0 – 0.19	Very weak	Little to no linear relationship
0.20 – 0.39	Weak	Some linear relationship, but not very strong
0.40 – 0.59	Moderate	Noticeable linear relationship
0.60 – 0.79	Strong	Strong linear relationship
0.80 – 0.99	Very strong	Very strong, near perfect linear relationship
1.00	Perfect	Exact linear relationship (either perfectly positive or perfectly negative)

The sign of r indicates the direction of the relationship.

- **Positive r**: Variables move in the same direction (e.g., as one increases, the other increases).
- **Negative r**: Variables move in opposite directions (e.g., as one increases, the other decreases).

Correlation does not imply causation. Just because two variables are correlated does not mean that one causes the other. Consider the sample size when interpreting r. Larger sample sizes tend to be more reliable.

Coefficient of determination:

It also known as R-squared or $r2$, is a measure of how well a statistical model fits the data. It is the proportion of the variation in the dependent variable that is explained by the independent variable(s) in the model. The value of $r2$ can range from 0 to 1, where 0 means no fit and 1 means perfect fit. A higher $r2$ indicates a better fit and a lower $r2$ indicates a worse fit. Coefficient of determination is a valuable tool in medical research for assessing model fit, evaluating treatment effectiveness, developing risk prediction models, advancing precision medicine, and optimizing resource allocation. It provides a quantitative measure of how well variables explain variability in health outcomes, contributing to more informed and effective decision-making in medical practice and research.

Chapter 9

Regression

Regression in statistics is a method of estimating the relationship between a dependent variable and one or more independent variables. It can be used to test hypotheses, predict outcomes, or explore associations between variables.

Regression analysis is used to explore the relationship between variables, such as how an exposure or treatment affects an outcome, or how to predict an outcome based on some factors. It can also help to adjust for confounding variables, deal with missing data, and detect outliers.

Types of Regression models:

Most common regression models in medical research are.

- **Linear regression**: This model is used when the outcome variable is continuous and the relationship between the outcome and the predictors is linear.
  For example, linear regression can be used to estimate the effect of blood pressure on the risk of stroke.

- **Logistic regression**: This model is used when the outcome variable is binary, meaning it has only two possible values, such as yes or no, alive, or dead, etc.
  For example, logistic regression can be used to estimate the odds of developing diabetes based on age, weight, and family history.

- **Cox proportional hazards regression**: This model is used when the outcome variable is the time until an event occurs, such as death, recurrence of disease, or recovery. This model can account for censoring, which means that some subjects may not experience the event during the study period or may be lost to follow-up.

For example, Cox regression can be used to compare the survival rates of patients who received different therapies for cancer.

Types Linear regression: The main types of linear regression are:

- **Simple Linear Regression**: This is the basic form of linear regression involving a single independent variable (predictor) and a single dependent variable. The relationship between the two variables is modelled using a straight line.
- **Multiple Linear Regression**: In this type, there are two or more independent variables. The model includes a linear combination of these variables to predict the dependent variable. The equation for multiple linear regression is more complex than that of simple linear regression.
- **Polynomial Regression**: Polynomial regression extends linear regression by incorporating polynomial terms of the independent variable(s) to capture nonlinear relationships. For example, a quadratic regression involves a squared term, and a cubic regression includes a cubed term.

Assumptions for Linear regression

- The relationship between the dependent variable and the independent variables is assumed to be linear.
- The residuals, which are the differences between the observed and predicted values, should be independent of each other.
- Homoscedasticity (Constant Variance of Residuals) – This assumption ensures that the spread of the residuals is consistent throughout the range of the independent variables.
- The residuals should be approximately normally distributed.
- No Perfect Multicollinearity.
- No Autocorrelation.
- Additivity – The effect of changes in an independent variable on the dependent variable is assumed to be constant across all levels of other independent variables.
- No Outliers or Influential Points: Extreme values or outliers in the data can unduly influence the regression coefficients.

The formula for linear regression equation is given by:

$$y = a + bx$$

where Y is the dependent variable (that's the variable that goes on the Y axis), X is the independent variable (i.e. it is plotted on the X axis), b is the slope of the line and a is the y-intercept.

$$a = \frac{[(\sum y)(\sum x^2) - (\sum x)(\sum xy)]}{[n(\sum x^2) - (\sum x)^2]}$$

$$b = \frac{[n(\sum xy) - (\sum x)(\sum y)]}{[n(\sum x^2) - (\sum x^2)]}$$

Regression line:

It is also known as a line of best fit, is a straight line that represents the relationship between a dependent variable (Y) and one or more independent variables (X) in a statistical model. The primary purpose of the regression line is to capture the general trend or pattern in the data and provide a means for making predictions. It is a versatile tool in medical research, aiding in outcome prediction, risk factor identification, dose-response analysis, clinical decision support, health economic studies, quality improvement initiatives, clinical trials, and patient stratification. Its application contributes to evidence-based medicine, enabling more informed decision-making for healthcare practitioners.

Types of logistic regressions:

The main types of linear regression are:

- **Binary Logistic Regression**: This is the most basic form of logistic regression, where the dependent variable has two categories or outcomes. It models the relationship between the independent variables and the probability of the event occurring.
- **Multinomial Logistic Regression**: When the dependent variable has more than two categories, multinomial logistic regression is used. It models the relationship between the independent variables and the probability of each category of the dependent variable.

- o **Ordinal Logistic Regression**: This type is suitable when the dependent variable is ordinal, meaning it has ordered categories but the intervals between categories are not assumed to be equal. Ordinal logistic regression models the cumulative odds of an observation falling into or below a particular category.
- o **Conditional Logistic Regression**: Conditional logistic regression is used in matched case-control studies, where each case is matched with one or more controls based on certain characteristics. It models the conditional probability of the outcome given the matched sets.

Assumptions for Logistic regression

- o The response variable is binary or ordinal, depending on the type of logistic regression (binary, multinomial, or ordinal).
- o The observations are independent of each other and not repeated or matched.
- o There is little or no multicollinearity among the predictor variables, meaning they are not highly correlated with each other.
- o The predictor variables are linearly related to the logit of the outcome variable, which is the natural logarithm of the odds ratio.
- o The sample size is large enough to ensure reliable estimates of the model parameters.

Summary of the differences between major types of regression model:

Type of Regression	Dependent Variable	Independent Variables
Simple Linear Regression	Continuous	One
Multiple Linear Regression	Continuous	Two or more
Polynomial Regression	Continuous	One or more
Logistic Regression	Categorical	One or more
Cox Proportional Hazards Regression	Survival time	One or more

Chapter 10

Manual on Statistical Analysis with SPSS

(Statistical Package for the Social Sciences)

As aspiring healthcare professionals, you are undoubtedly aware of the critical role that data analysis plays in medical research, clinical practice, and evidence-based decision-making. Understanding statistical concepts and being proficient in data analysis tools like SPSS are essential skills that will empower you to contribute meaningfully to medical research and practice.

In this chapter, we will embark on a journey to explore the fundamental concepts of SPSS and its practical applications in the context of medical research and clinical studies. We recognize that many medical students may be relatively new to statistical analysis software like SPSS, and thus, this chapter aims to provide a comprehensive yet accessible guide to help you navigate through the complexities of SPSS.

Before delving into the intricacies of SPSS, let's take a moment to understand the significance of statistical analysis in the field of medicine. In the ever-evolving landscape of healthcare, medical research serves as the foundation for advancements in diagnosis, treatment, and patient care. From clinical trials evaluating the efficacy of new drugs to epidemiological studies investigating disease prevalence and risk factors, statistical analysis lies at the heart of medical research endeavors.

As future healthcare providers, it is imperative for you to be able to critically evaluate research findings, interpret statistical data, and apply evidence-based practices in clinical settings. Mastery of statistical analysis tools like SPSS equips you with the necessary skills to engage with medical literature, conduct your research projects, and contribute to the advancement of medical knowledge.

Now, let's turn our attention to SPSS, a versatile software package that facilitates data management, statistical analysis, and data visualization. Originally developed in the 1960s by Norman H. Nie and his colleagues at Stanford University, SPSS has since become one of the most widely used statistical analysis tools across various disciplines, including medicine, psychology, sociology, and economics.

SPSS offers a user-friendly interface and a wide range of features designed to streamline the process of data analysis. Whether you are performing basic descriptive statistics, conducting complex statistical analyses, or creating informative graphs and charts, SPSS provides the tools you need to explore and interpret your data effectively.

In this chapter, we will cover a broad spectrum of topics related to SPSS, starting with the basics of data entry and management. We will walk you through the process of importing data into SPSS, defining variables, and organizing your dataset for analysis. Understanding how to structure and manage your data is crucial for ensuring accuracy and reliability in your analyses.

Once you have mastered the fundamentals of data management, we will delve into the realm of descriptive statistics. Descriptive statistics allow you to summarize and explore the characteristics of your data, providing valuable insights into central tendency, variability, and distribution. We will discuss how to calculate measures such as mean, median, mode, standard deviation, and variance using SPSS.

Moving beyond descriptive statistics, we will explore inferential statistics, which enable you to draw conclusions and make predictions based on sample data. From hypothesis testing to regression analysis, we will demonstrate how SPSS can be used to Analyse relationships between variables, test for differences between groups, and assess the significance of findings.

Throughout this chapter, we will emphasize the importance of data integrity, ethical considerations, and best practices in statistical analysis. Medical research carries significant implications for patient care and public health, and as future healthcare professionals, it is essential to conduct research ethically and responsibly.

In addition to statistical analysis, SPSS offers powerful tools for data visualization, allowing you to present your findings in a clear and compelling manner. We will explore the various chart types, graphs, and plots available in SPSS and discuss how to customize them to effectively communicate your results.

Furthermore, we will address common challenges and pitfalls that may arise during data analysis and provide strategies for troubleshooting and problem-solving. Whether you encounter missing data, outliers, or skewed distributions, we will equip you with the skills to handle these issues effectively and ensure the integrity of your analyses.

As you progress through this chapter, we encourage you to actively engage with the material, practice using SPSS with sample datasets, and explore its features and functionalities. Hands-on experience is invaluable for gaining proficiency in statistical analysis, and we aim to provide you with ample opportunities to apply what you learn in real-world scenarios.

In conclusion, this chapter is designed to empower medical students with the knowledge and skills necessary to excel in statistical analysis and research. By mastering SPSS, you will enhance your ability to critically evaluate medical literature, conduct research projects, and make evidence-based decisions in clinical practice. I hope that this chapter serves as a valuable resource on your journey towards becoming knowledgeable and proficient healthcare professionals. Let's embark on this learning adventure together and unlock the transformative potential of statistical analysis in medicine.

Downloading SPSS: A Step-by-Step Guide

1. **Downloading SPSS**:

   To download SPSS, you first need to visit the official IBM SPSS website or authorized vendors. There, you'll find various versions of SPSS available for purchase or trial. Follow these steps to download SPSS:

   a) Choose the appropriate version of SPSS based on your operating system (Windows or macOS) and requirements.

b) Click on the download link and follow the prompts to start the download process.

c) Once the download is complete, locate the downloaded file on your computer and double-click to begin the installation process.

d) Follow the installation wizard's instructions to install SPSS on your computer. Make sure to choose the appropriate options, such as the installation directory and additional features, as per your preferences.

2. **Activating SPSS**:

After installing SPSS, you'll need to activate it using a valid license key. If you've purchased a license, you should have received a license key via email or through your vendor. Follow these steps to activate SPSS:

a) Open SPSS on your computer. You'll be prompted to enter the license key during the activation process.

b) Enter the license key when prompted and follow the on-screen instructions to complete the activation process.

c) Once activated, you'll have access to the full functionality of SPSS and can start using it for data analysis.

Types of data files in SPSS

In SPSS, there are primarily three types of data files that are commonly used:

1. **Data files (.sav)**: These are the main data files used in SPSS. They contain the actual data that you input or import into SPSS for analysis. Data files have a ".sav" extension and can store both the data values and variable information.

2. **Syntax files (.sps)**: Syntax files contain commands written in the SPSS syntax language. They are used to automate tasks, perform complex analyses, and reproduce analyses consistently. Syntax files have a ".sps" extension and can be created and edited within the SPSS program or using a text editor.

3. **Output files (.spv, .spo)**: Output files contain the results of analyses performed in SPSS. They include tables, charts, and statistical summaries generated by SPSS. Output files can be saved in different

formats, such as ".spv" for viewer files or ".spo" for portable output files, and can be viewed, printed, or exported for further analysis or report.

Data files (.sav):

In SPSS, two primary interfaces are utilized:

- The **Data Editor Window**: This interface displays the dataset in two formats – the **Data View** for the data itself and the **Variable View** for the metadata about the variables.
- The **Output Viewer Window**: This is where the outcomes of statistical analyses are presented.

The **Data Editor Window – Data View**

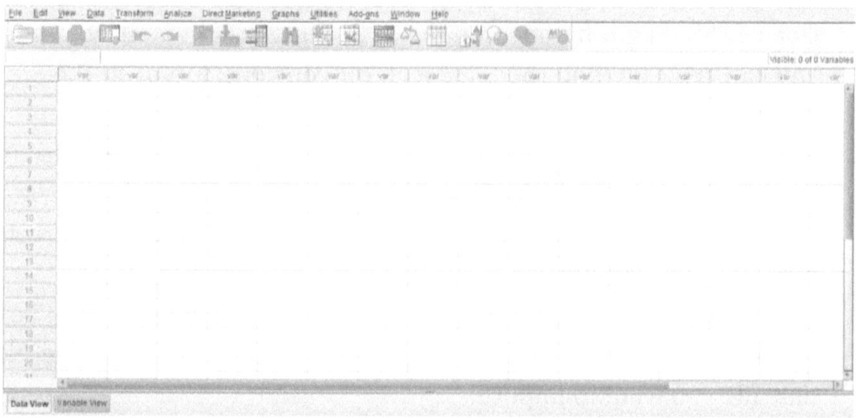

The Data Editor Window – Variable View

The Output Viewer Window

How to import data from Excel to SPSS?

1. Open SPSS: Begin by opening the SPSS software on your computer. You can typically find the SPSS icon on your desktop or in the Start menu.

2. Open a New or Existing Syntax File (Optional): If you prefer to use syntax to import the Excel file, you can open a new or existing syntax file. This step is optional, as you can also import the Excel file directly from the SPSS interface.

3. Go to File > Open > Data...: In the SPSS menu bar, navigate to File > Open > Data... This will open a dialog box where you can select the data file you want to import.

4. Select Excel (.xls, .xlsx) as the File Type: In the "Open Data" dialog box, make sure to select "Excel (*.xls, *.xlsx, *.xlsm)" as the file type from the dropdown menu. This ensures that SPSS recognizes Excel files when browsing for them.

5. Navigate to the Location of the Excel File: Use the file browser to navigate to the location on your computer where the Excel file is stored. Once you've located the file, select it by clicking on it, and then click "Open" to proceed.

6. Specify Import Options: After selecting the Excel file, SPSS will open the "Import Data" dialog box, where you can specify import options. Here, you can choose whether to import the entire worksheet or

select specific ranges of cells. You can also specify how to handle variable names, data types, and other import settings.

7. Review Variable Properties (Optional): If you're importing data into an existing SPSS dataset, SPSS may prompt you to review the variable properties before proceeding with the import. You can modify variable names, labels, and other properties as needed.

8. Complete the Import Process: Once you've specified the import options and reviewed the variable properties (if applicable), click "OK" or "Finish" to complete the import process. SPSS will then import the Excel file into the active dataset or create a new dataset, depending on your selection.

9. Verify Data Import: After importing the Excel file, take a moment to verify that the data has been imported correctly. You can inspect the data in the Data View or Variable View tabs of the SPSS interface to ensure accuracy.

10. Save Your SPSS Dataset (Optional): Finally, consider saving your SPSS dataset (.sav file) to preserve the imported data and any modifications you've made. Go to File > Save As... and choose a location and filename for your SPSS dataset.

How to define variables in SPSS?

1. Open a New or Existing Data File: If you're starting a new analysis, open a new data file by going to File > New > Data. Alternatively, if you're working with an existing data file, open it by going to File > Open > Data...

2. Access Variable View: Once the data file is open, navigate to the "Variable View" tab located at the bottom of the SPSS interface. Click on the "Variable View" tab to switch to the Variable View mode.

3. Enter Variable Names: In the first column of the Variable View, you'll see a list of variable names (e.g., Var1, Var2, Var3). Double-click on each variable name cell to edit it and enter a descriptive name for each variable. Variable names should be concise and meaningful, reflecting the data they represent (e.g., Age, Gender, Income).

4. Enter Variable Labels (Optional): In the second column of the Variable View, you can enter variable labels to provide additional description or context for each variable. Double-click on each cell

in the Label column to add or edit the variable label. Variable labels are helpful for clarifying the meaning of variables, especially when sharing or documenting data.

5. Specify Variable Type: In the third column of the Variable View, you'll find the "Type" column. This column allows you to specify the type of data each variable represents. Click on the cell in the Type column corresponding to each variable to select the appropriate data type:

    Numeric: For variables that represent numerical data (e.g., age, weight).

    String: For variables that represent text or alphanumeric data (e.g., names, addresses).

    Date: For variables that represent dates or times.

6. Specify Variable Width and Decimals (Numeric Variables): For numeric variables, you can specify the width (maximum number of characters) and the number of decimal places to display. Click on the cells in the "Width" and "Decimals" columns to enter the desired values.

7. Define Value Labels (Optional): Value labels allow you to assign meaningful labels to numeric codes or categories within a variable. To define value labels, click on the "Values" cell corresponding to each variable and enter the numeric codes and their corresponding labels in the "Value Label" dialog box.

8. Enter Missing Values (Optional): If your dataset includes missing or invalid data values, you can specify them as missing values for each variable. Click on the "Missing" cell corresponding to each variable and enter the codes or ranges representing missing values.

9. Repeat for Each Variable: Repeat steps 4-9 for each variable in your dataset, ensuring that each variable is properly defined with a name, label, type, width, and any additional properties (e.g., value labels, missing values).

10. Switch to Data View: Once you've defined all variables in the Variable View, switch back to the "Data View" tab to enter or import your data into the dataset. You can toggle between the Variable View and Data View tabs at any time to modify variable properties or view the data.

How to convert a continuous variable to categories in SPSS?

Converting a continuous variable into categories in SPSS is a common data pre-processing step that allows researchers to analyse data more effectively. This process, known as binning or categorization, involves grouping continuous data into discrete categories based on predefined criteria.

1. Open SPSS and Load Data: Start by opening SPSS and loading the dataset containing the continuous variable you want to convert into categories. You can either open an existing SPSS data file (.sav) or import data from an external source.

2. Identify Continuous Variable: Identify the continuous variable in your dataset that you want to convert into categories. For example, let's consider a dataset containing information about the heights of individuals.

3. Define Categories: Determine the criteria for categorizing the continuous variable into discrete categories. This can be based on domain knowledge, statistical considerations, or specific research objectives. For example, you might decide to categorize heights into short, average, and tall categories.

4. Create a New Categorical Variable: In SPSS, you'll need to create a new variable to store the categorical values. Go to the "Variable View" tab and locate an empty row at the bottom of the variable list. Double-click on the cell under the "Name" column to enter a name for the new variable (e.g., Height Category).

5. Define Value Labels for Categories: In the "Value Labels" column of the new categorical variable, define labels for each category. For example, you might assign labels "Short," "Average," and "Tall" to the respective categories.

6. Switch to Data View: Once you've defined the new categorical variable, switch to the "Data View" tab to enter or calculate the values for the new variable based on the categories you defined.

7. Assign Categories to Continuous Variable: Use the "Recode into Different Variables" or "Compute Variable" option in SPSS to assign categories to the continuous variable based on the defined criteria.

For example, you can use the "IF" function in the "Compute Variable" dialog box to assign values to the new categorical variable based on the ranges of the continuous variable.

In this example, individuals with heights less than 160 cm are categorized as "Short" (Category 1), those with heights between 160 cm and 170 cm are categorized as "Average" (Category 2), and those with heights greater than 170 cm are categorized as "Tall" (Category 3).

8. Execute and Verify: Execute the syntax or calculations to assign categories to the continuous variable. Switch back to the "Variable View" or "Data View" tab to verify that the new categorical variable has been created and populated correctly.

9. Analyse Data: Once the continuous variable has been converted into categories, you can use the new categorical variable for data analysis. You can perform analyses such as frequency distributions, cross-tabulations, and chi-square tests to explore relationships between the categorical variable and other variables in the dataset.

How to Transform variables – Recode into different variables in SPSS

Transforming variables by recoding into different variables is a common operation in SPSS, allowing you to create new variables based on existing ones with modified values.

1. Open SPSS and Load Data: Start by opening SPSS and loading the dataset containing the variable you want to recode into different variables. You can either open an existing SPSS data file (.sav) or import data from an external source.

2. Identify Variable to Recode: Identify the variable in your dataset that you want to transform by recoding into different variables. For example, let's consider a dataset containing information about respondents' ages.

3. Define Recoding Criteria: Determine the criteria for recoding the variable into different categories or values. This can be based on specific research questions, statistical considerations, or domain

knowledge. For example, you might decide to recode ages into different age groups.

4. Access Transform > Recode into Different Variables: In SPSS, go to the "Transform" menu in the menu bar and select "Recode into Different Variables..." This will open the "Recode into Different Variables" dialog box.

5. Select Variable to Recode: In the "Recode into Different Variables" dialog box, select the variable you want to recode from the list of available variables in the "Input Variable" section. Click on the variable name to move it to the "Input Variable" box.

6. Create New Variable Name: Specify a name for the new variable that will store the recoded values. Enter the desired name in the "Name" field under the "Output Variable" section. This will be the name of the new variable that you create.

7. Define Recoding Rules: In the "Recode" section of the dialog box, define the recoding rules or criteria for transforming the values of the input variable into new values for the output variable. You can specify different recoding options, including range, exact value, or missing values.

> Example Recoding Criteria: Let's say we want to recode ages into three age groups:
>> Age < 30: Recode to "Young"
>> Age 30-59: Recode to "Adult"
>> Age ≥ 60: Recode to "Senior"

8. Add Recoding Rules: Click on the "Old" button to define the original values of the input variable, and then specify the corresponding new values for each category or range. You can add multiple recoding rules to cover different conditions or categories.

> Example Recoding Rules:
>> Old: 0 THRU 29 New: "Young"
>> Old: 30 THRU 59 New: "Adult"
>> Old: 60 THRU HIGHEST New: "Senior"

9. Review and Verify: Review the recoding rules to ensure they accurately reflect the transformation you want to apply. You can preview the

recoded values in the "Output Variable" section to verify that the transformation is correct.

10. Execute Transformation: Once you're satisfied with the recoding rules, click "OK" to execute the transformation. SPSS will create a new variable with the specified name and recoded values based on the defined criteria.

11. Verify Output: Switch to the "Data View" or "Variable View" tab to verify that the new variable has been created and populated with the recoded values. You can inspect the values of the new variable to ensure they match the desired transformation.

How to use Compute Function in SPSS?

Using the Compute function in SPSS allows you to create new variables by performing calculations or transformations on existing variables.

1. Open SPSS and Load Data: Start by opening SPSS and loading the dataset containing the variables you want to work with. You can either open an existing SPSS data file (.sav) or import data from an external source.

2. Identify Variables: Identify the variables in your dataset that you want to use in the computation. These can be existing variables or new variables that you'll create as part of the computation.

3. Access Transform > Compute Variable: In SPSS, go to the "Transform" menu in the menu bar and select "Compute Variable..." This will open the "Compute Variable" dialog box.

4. Specify Target Variable Name: In the "Target Variable" field of the "Compute Variable" dialog box, enter a name for the new variable that will store the computed values. This will be the name of the variable you create through the computation.

5. Enter Computation Formula: In the "Numeric Expression" field of the dialog box, enter the computation formula that defines how the new variable will be calculated. You can use mathematical operators (+, −, *, /), functions, and references to existing variables in the formula.

   Example Computation Formula: Let's say we want to compute Body Mass Index (BMI) using the formula: BMI = weight (kg) / (height (m))^2

6. Specify Existing Variables: If the computation formula references existing variables in the dataset, make sure to select them from the list of available variables in the dialog box. You can either double-click on the variable names or drag them into the "Numeric Expression" field to include them in the computation.

   Example:
   Select the "weight" variable from the list and click the arrow button to insert it into the expression.
   Similarly, select the "height" variable and insert it into the expression.

7. Review and Verify: Review the computation formula to ensure it accurately reflects the calculation you want to perform. You can use the "Paste" button to insert variable names and operators into the expression field, ensuring accuracy.

8. Execute Computation: Once you're satisfied with the computation formula, click "OK" to execute the computation. SPSS will create a new variable with the specified name and values based on the computation formula.

9. Verify Output: Switch to the "Data View" or "Variable View" tab to verify that the new variable has been created and populated with the computed values. You can inspect the values of the new variable to ensure they match the expected results based on the computation formula.

How to do descriptive statistics for a continuous variable using SPSS?

To perform descriptive statistics for a continuous variable using SPSS, follow these steps:

1. Open SPSS: Launch the SPSS software on your computer.

2. Import Data: If your data is not already loaded into SPSS, you'll need to import it. Go to "File" > "Open" to navigate to your data file and open it.

3. Variable View: In the SPSS Data Editor window, click on the "Variable View" tab at the bottom.

4. Define Variable: Enter a name for your continuous variable in the first row under the "Name" column. Specify the type of measurement (numeric) in the "Type" column.
5. Enter Data: Switch to the "Data View" tab and enter your data values for the continuous variable in the corresponding column.
6. Analyse Menu: Go to the "Analyse" menu at the top of the SPSS window.
7. Descriptive Statistics: From the "Analyse" menu, select "Descriptive Statistics" and then choose "Descriptives."
8. Select Variable: In the "Descriptives" dialog box, move your continuous variable from the list of available variables to the list of variables to be Analysed by clicking on the variable name and then clicking the arrow button pointing to the right.
9. Options: If you want specific statistics, such as mean, median, standard deviation, minimum, maximum, etc., click on the "Options" button and check the boxes next to the statistics you want to include.
10. Click "OK": Once you've selected your variable and any desired options, click the "OK" button to run the analysis.
11. View Results: SPSS will generate output in the Output Viewer window, displaying the descriptive statistics for your continuous variable. You can view the mean, standard deviation, minimum, maximum, and other statistics you selected.
12. Save Output: If you want to save the results, go to "File" > "Save As" and choose a file format to save the output.

How to do descriptive statistics for a categorical variable using SPSS?

To perform descriptive statistics for a categorical variable using SPSS, you can use frequency analysis. Here's a step-by-step guide:

1. Open SPSS and Import Data: Launch SPSS and open your dataset containing the categorical variable you want to Analyse.
2. Analyse Menu: Go to the "Analyse" menu at the top of the SPSS window.
3. Descriptive Statistics: From the "Analyse" menu, navigate to "Descriptive Statistics" and then select "Frequencies."

4. Select Variable: In the "Frequencies" dialog box, you will see a list of variables from your dataset. Select the categorical variable you want to Analyse and move it into the "Variable(s)" box.
5. Options (Optional): You can click on the "Statistics" button to request additional statistics, such as mean, median, mode, range, etc., for any numeric variables in your dataset. You can also click on the "Charts" button to request graphical representations of your data, such as bar charts.
6. Click "OK": Once you've selected your variable and any desired options, click the "OK" button to run the analysis.
7. Interpret Results: SPSS will generate output in the Output Viewer window, which includes a frequency table for your categorical variable. The frequency table displays the categories of the variable along with the frequency count and percentage for each category.
8. Optional: Charts (Bar Charts): If you requested bar charts, SPSS would also generate graphical representations of your data, showing the distribution of your categorical variable. You can use these charts to visualize the frequency distribution of each category.
9. Save Output (Optional): If you want to save the results, go to "File" > "Save As" and choose a file format to save the output.

How to do descriptive statistics for association between 2 categorical variables using SPSS? (Example: gender and type of diabetes)

To perform descriptive statistics for the association between two categorical variables using SPSS, you can use the Crosstabs procedure. Here's a step-by-step guide:

1. Open SPSS and Import Data: Launch SPSS and open your dataset containing the two categorical variables you want to Analyse (e.g., gender and type of diabetes).
2. Analyse Menu: Go to the "Analyse" menu at the top of the SPSS window.
3. Descriptive Statistics: From the "Analyse" menu, navigate to "Descriptive Statistics" and then select "Crosstabs."
4. Select Variables: In the "Crosstabs" dialog box, you will see a list of variables from your dataset. Select the variable representing gender

and move it into the "Row(s)" box. Similarly, select the variable representing the type of diabetes and move it into the "Column(s)" box.

5. You can click on the "Statistics" button to request additional statistics, such as chi-square, measures of association (e.g., Cramer's V), etc. You can also click on the "Cells" button to specify whether you want row percentages, column percentages, or both in your output.

6. Once you've selected your variables and any desired options, click the "OK" button to run the analysis.

7. Interpret Results: SPSS will generate output in the Output Viewer window, which includes a contingency table showing the frequencies and percentages of each combination of categories for the two variables. You can Analyse this table to understand the relationship between the two categorical variables. For example, you can examine whether the distribution of diabetes types varies by gender.

8. If you requested the chi-square statistic, SPSS will also provide the results of the chi-square test, which assesses the association between the two categorical variables. You can use this test to determine whether the association is statistically significant.

9. Save Output (Optional): If you want to save the results, go to "File" > "Save As" and choose a file format to save the output.

How to do Normality test in SPSS?

To perform a normality test in SPSS, you can use the Shapiro-Wilk test or the Kolmogorov-Smirnov test.

1. Launch SPSS and open the dataset containing the variable for which you want to test normality.

2. Go to the "Analyse" menu at the top of the SPSS window.

3. From the "Analyse" menu, select "Descriptive Statistics" and then click on "Explore."

4. In the "Explore" dialog box, move the variable for which you want to test normality to the "Dependent List" box.

5. You can specify additional options under the "Plots" and "Statistics" buttons if you want to generate plots or obtain specific statistics. For normality testing, you generally don't need to change these options.

6. Click the "OK" button to run the Explore procedure.
7. SPSS will generate output containing various statistics and plots. Look for the Shapiro-Wilk test or the Kolmogorov-Smirnov test in the "Normality Tests" section of the output. If you used Shapiro-Wilk, focus on the p-value associated with the test. If the p-value is greater than the significance level (e.g., 0.05), it indicates that the data is normally distributed. If the p-value is less than the significance level, it suggests departure from normality.
8. If you used Kolmogorov-Smirnov, look at the "Sig." (Significance) column. A non-significant result (p > 0.05) suggests normality.

How to compare the difference in mean of a continuous variable from a standard value using SPSS?

Compare the mean Fasting blood sugar (FBS)of patients with a standard value which is obtained from textbook or a guideline.

To compare the difference in the mean of a continuous variable (e.g., Fasting Blood Sugar – FBS) from a standard value using SPSS, you can conduct a one-sample t-test.

1. Launch SPSS and open your dataset containing the FBS values of patients.
2. Go to the "Analyse" menu at the top of the SPSS window.
3. From the "Analyse" menu, navigate to "Compare Means" and then select "One-Sample T Test."
4. In the "One-Sample T Test" dialog box, you will see a list of variables from your dataset. Select the variable representing FBS and move it into the "Test Variable(s)" box.
5. In the "Test Value" box, enter the standard value obtained from the textbook or guideline. This value represents the population mean or standard that you want to compare your sample mean against.
6. You can click on the "Options" button to specify any additional settings or statistics you want to include in your output. For example, you can request descriptive statistics or confidence intervals.
7. Once you've selected your variable and entered the test value, click the "OK" button to run the analysis.

8. SPSS will generate output in the Output Viewer window, which includes the results of the one-sample t-test. Look for the "t" value and associated p-value in the output. The "t" value indicates the difference between the sample mean and the test value in terms of standard error units, while the p-value indicates the significance of this difference. If the p-value is less than your chosen significance level (e.g., 0.05), you can conclude that there is a statistically significant difference between the sample mean and the test value.

9. If you want to save the results, go to "File" > "Save As" and choose a file format to save the output.

How to compare the difference in means of continuous variable from 2 different groups (2 independent groups) using SPSS?

Compare Systolic blood pressure of two interventional drug groups – Group A and Group B.

To compare the difference in means of a continuous variable between two independent groups using SPSS, such as comparing the systolic blood pressure of two interventional drug groups (Group A and Group B), you can perform an independent samples t-test.

1. Launch SPSS and open your dataset containing the systolic blood pressure measurements for both Group A and Group B.
2. Go to the "Analyse" menu at the top of the SPSS window.
3. From the "Analyse" menu, navigate to "Compare Means" and then select "Independent Samples T-Test."
4. In the "Independent Samples T Test" dialog box, you will see a list of variables from your dataset. Select the variable representing systolic blood pressure and move it into the "Test Variable(s)" box. Next, select the variable representing the group (e.g., Group A and Group B) and move it into the "Grouping Variable" box.
5. Click on the "Define Groups" button to specify the coding for your groups. For example, if Group A is coded as 1 and Group B is coded as 2, enter these values in the corresponding boxes.

6. You can click on the "Options" button to request additional statistics, such as confidence intervals for the mean difference, effect size measures (e.g., Cohen's d), etc.

7. Once you've selected your variables and any desired options, click the "OK" button to run the analysis.

8. SPSS will generate output in the Output Viewer window, which includes various statistics such as means, standard deviations, t-values, degrees of freedom, and p-values. Focus on the p-value associated with the independent samples t-test.

    a) This p-value indicates whether there is a statistically significant difference in the mean systolic blood pressure between Group A and Group B.

    b) If the p-value is less than your chosen significance level (e.g., 0.05), you can conclude that there is a statistically significant difference in the mean systolic blood pressure between the two groups.

9. To save the results, go to "File" > "Save As" and choose a file format to save the output.

How to compare the difference in means of paired data using SPSS?

Compare the mean fasting blood sugar (FBS) of patients before and after treatment.

1. Ensure that you have a dataset with two columns: one for the FBS measurements before treatment and another for FBS measurements after treatment. Each row represents a patient.

2. Launch SPSS and open the dataset containing the FBS measurements.

3. Go to the "Analyse" menu at the top of the SPSS window.

4. From the "Analyse" menu, select "Compare Means" and then click on "Paired-Samples T Test."

5. In the "Paired-Samples T Test" dialog box, you will see a list of variables. Move the variable representing FBS before treatment to the box labelled "Paired Variables" on the left side, and the variable representing FBS after treatment to the box labelled "Paired Variables" on the right side.

6. If needed, you can specify additional options such as confidence intervals and descriptive statistics by clicking on the "Options" button.
7. Click the "OK" button to run the paired-samples t-test.
8. SPSS will generate output containing various statistics, including the mean difference between paired observations, standard deviation, t-value, degrees of freedom, and p-value.
9. Focus on the p-value associated with the t-test. If the p-value is less than the significance level (e.g., 0.05), it indicates a statistically significant difference in means between the two paired groups.

How to compare the difference in means of continuous data from more than 2 groups using SPSS?

Compare Body Mass Index (BMI) of different age groups.

To compare the difference in means of continuous data from more than two groups using SPSS, you can use analysis of variance (ANOVA).

1. Ensure you have a dataset with the Body Mass Index (BMI) measurements for different age groups. Each row represents an individual with their corresponding BMI and age group.
2. Launch SPSS and open the dataset containing BMI measurements for different age groups.
3. Go to the "Analyse" menu at the top of the SPSS window.
4. From the "Analyse" menu, select "Compare Means" and then click on "One-Way ANOVA."
5. In the "One-Way ANOVA" dialog box, you will see a list of variables. Move the variable representing BMI to the "Dependent List" box.
6. Move the variable representing age groups to the "Factor" box. This defines the groups for which you want to compare the mean BMI.
7. If needed, you can specify additional options such as descriptive statistics and post hoc tests by clicking on the "Options" button.
8. Click the "OK" button to run the ANOVA analysis.
9. SPSS will generate output containing various statistics, including the F-value, degrees of freedom, and p-value. Focus on the p-value

associated with the ANOVA test. If the p-value is less than the significance level (e.g., 0.05), it indicates a statistically significant difference in mean BMI across different age groups. If the ANOVA test shows a significant difference, you can perform post hoc tests (e.g., Tukey's HSD) to identify which specific age groups differ significantly in mean BMI.

How to study the association between 2 categorical variables using SPSS?

To study the association between levels of Diabetes mellitus with different grades of BMI.

1. Launch SPSS and open the dataset containing the variables for Diabetes mellitus and BMI.
2. Go to the "Analyse" menu at the top of the SPSS window.
3. From the "Analyse" menu, select "Descriptive Statistics" and then click on "Crosstabs."
4. In the "Crosstabs" dialog box, move the variable for Diabetes mellitus to the "Row(s)" box, and the variable for BMI to the "Column(s)" box.
5. You can specify additional statistics to be calculated by clicking on the "Statistics" button. For studying association, you generally don't need to change these options.
6. Click the "OK" button to run the Crosstabs procedure.
7. SPSS will generate a Crosstabs table showing the frequencies and percentages of each combination of categories for the two variables. Look at the cells of the Crosstabs table to observe the distribution of cases across different categories. To assess the association between Diabetes mellitus and BMI, look at the Chi-square test statistic and its associated p-value in the "Chi-Square Tests" section of the output. If the p-value is less than the significance level (e.g., 0.05), it indicates that there is a significant association between Diabetes mellitus and BMI categories.

How to check if the difference in a continuous variable from a standard value is statistically significant, if the data is not normally distributed?

Compare the mean Fasting blood sugar (FBS)of patients with a standard value which is obtained from textbook or a guideline.

To compare the difference in a continuous variable from a standard value when the data is not normally distributed, you can use Wilcoxon signed-rank test.

1. Launch SPSS and open the dataset containing the Fasting blood sugar (FBS) values.
2. Go to the "Analyse" menu at the top of the SPSS window.
3. From the "Analyse" menu, select "Nonparametric Tests" and then click on "Related Samples."
4. In the "Related Samples" dialog box, move the variable for FBS to the "Test Variable List."
5. If you have a specific standard value obtained from a textbook or guideline, you can enter it in the "Test Value" field. Otherwise, leave it blank.
6. Select "Wilcoxon" from the list of non-parametric tests.
7. Click the "OK" button to run the Wilcoxon signed-rank test.
8. SPSS will generate output showing the test statistics, including the Z value and the associated p-value. Look at the p-value to determine if the difference between the FBS values and the standard value is statistically significant. If the p-value is less than the significance level (e.g., 0.05), it indicates a significant difference between the FBS values and the standard value.

How to compare the difference in continuous variable from 2 different groups (2 independent groups) using SPSS, if the data is not normally distributed?

Compare Systolic blood pressure of two interventional drug groups – Group A and Group B.

To compare the difference in a continuous variable from two different groups (two independent groups) when the data is not normally distributed, you can use Mann-Whitney U test.

1. Launch SPSS and open the dataset containing the Systolic blood pressure values for Group A and Group B.
2. Go to the "Analyse" menu at the top of the SPSS window.
3. From the "Analyse" menu, select "Nonparametric Tests" and then click on "Independent Samples."
4. In the "Independent Samples" dialog box, move the Systolic blood pressure variable to the "Test Variable List" and the Group variable (indicating Group A and Group B) to the "Grouping Variable" box.
5. Click on the "Options" button to specify the test options. In the "Options" dialog box, make sure "Mann-Whitney U" is selected as the test to perform.
6. Click the "Continue" button to return to the "Independent Samples Test" dialog box. Click the "OK" button to run the Mann-Whitney U test.
7. SPSS will generate output showing the test statistics, including the U value and the associated p-value. Look at the p-value to determine if the difference in Systolic blood pressure between Group A and Group B is statistically significant. If the p-value is less than the significance level (e.g., 0.05), it indicates a significant difference between the two groups.

How to compare the difference in paired data or related data using SPSS, if data is not normally distributed?

Compare the mean fasting blood sugar (FBS) of patients before and after treatment.

To compare the difference in paired data or related data when the data is not normally distributed, you can use Wilcoxon signed-rank test.

1. Launch SPSS and open the dataset containing the fasting blood sugar (FBS) values for patients before and after treatment.
2. Go to the "Analyse" menu at the top of the SPSS window.
3. From the "Analyse" menu, select "Nonparametric Tests" and then click on "Legacy Dialogs."
4. In the "Legacy Dialogs" submenu, click on "2 Related Samples."
5. In the "2 Related Samples" dialog box, move the fasting blood sugar variable (FBS) to the "Test Variable List. Ensure that the variable

indicating "Before Treatment" is listed first, followed by the variable indicating "After Treatment."

6. Click on the "Options" button to specify the test options. In the "Options" dialog box, make sure "Wilcoxon" is selected as the test to perform.

7. Click the "OK" button to run the Wilcoxon signed-rank test.

8. SPSS will generate output showing the test statistics, including the test statistic (Z or W value) and the associated p-value. Look at the p-value to determine if the difference in fasting blood sugar before and after treatment is statistically significant. If the p-value is less than the significance level (e.g., 0.05), it indicates a significant difference in FBS levels before and after treatment.

How to compare the difference in means of continuous data from more than 2 groups using SPSS, if data is not normally distributed?

Compare Body Mass Index (BMI) of different age groups.

To compare the difference in means of continuous data from more than two groups, especially when the data is not normally distributed, you can use Kruskal-Wallis test.

1. Launch SPSS and open the dataset containing the Body Mass Index (BMI) values for different age groups.

2. Go to the "Analyse" menu at the top of the SPSS window.

3. From the "Analyse" menu, select "Nonparametric Tests" and then click on "Legacy Dialogs."

4. In the "Legacy Dialogs" submenu, click on "K Independent Samples."

5. In the "K Independent Samples" dialog box, move the BMI variable to the "Test Variable List." Move the variable indicating different age groups to the "Grouping Variable" box.

6. Click on the "Options" button to specify the test options. In the "Options" dialog box, ensure that "Kruskal-Wallis H" is selected as the test to perform.

7. Click the "OK" button to run the Kruskal-Wallis test.

8. SPSS will generate output showing the test statistics, including the test statistic (H value) and the associated p-value. Look at the p-value to determine if there is a statistically significant difference in BMI among the different age groups. If the p-value is less than the chosen significance level (e.g., 0.05), it indicates that there is a significant difference in BMI among at least two age groups.

How to measure of the strength and direction of linear relationship that exists between two continuous variables using SPSS and the variables are normally distributed?

Measure the strength and direction of Fasting blood sugar level (FBS) and Body Mass Index (BMI).

To measure the strength and direction of the linear relationship between two continuous variables, such as Fasting Blood Sugar (FBS) level and Body Mass Index (BMI), you can use Pearson's correlation coefficient in SPSS.

1. Launch SPSS and open the dataset containing the FBS and BMI values.
2. Go to the "Analyse" menu at the top of the SPSS window.
3. From the "Analyse" menu, select "Correlate" and then click on "Bivariate."
4. In the "Bivariate Correlations" dialog box, move the FBS variable to the "Variables" box. Move the BMI variable to the "Variables" box as well.
5. Under "Correlation Coefficient," make sure "Pearson" is selected. Pearson's correlation coefficient is used to measure linear relationships between continuous variables.
6. Click the "OK" button to run the correlation analysis.
7. SPSS will generate output showing the correlation coefficient (r) between FBS and BMI, along with its significance level (p-value). The correlation coefficient (r) ranges from -1 to 1. A value close to 1 indicates a strong positive linear relationship (as one variable increases, the other also increases). A value close to -1 indicates a strong negative linear relationship (as one variable increases, the other decreases). A value close to 0 indicates a weak or no linear

relationship between the variables. The p-value indicates the statistical significance of the correlation coefficient. If the p-value is less than the chosen significance level (e.g., 0.05), the correlation is considered statistically significant.

How to measure of the strength and direction of linear relationship that exists between two continuous variables using SPSS and the variables are not normally distributed?

Measure the strength and direction of Systolic blood pressure and Triglyceride level.

To measure the strength and direction of the linear relationship between two continuous variables using SPSS when the variables are not normally distributed, you can use Spearman's rank correlation coefficient.

8. Launch SPSS and open the dataset containing the Systolic Blood Pressure and Triglyceride level values.
9. Go to the "Analyse" menu at the top of the SPSS window.
10. From the "Analyse" menu, select "Correlate" and then click on "Bivariate."
11. In the "Bivariate Correlations" dialog box, move the Systolic Blood Pressure variable to the "Variables" box. Move the Triglyceride level variable to the "Variables" box as well.
12. Under "Correlation Coefficient," select "Spearman" from the drop-down menu. Spearman's rank correlation coefficient is used when the variables are not normally distributed.
13. Click the "OK" button to run the correlation analysis.
14. SPSS will generate output showing the Spearman correlation coefficient (rho) between Systolic Blood Pressure and Triglyceride level, along with its significance level (p-value). The correlation coefficient (rho) ranges from – 1 to 1. A value close to 1 indicates a strong positive monotonic relationship (as one variable increases, the other tends to increase). A value close to – 1 indicates a strong negative monotonic relationship (as one variable 9increases, the other tends to decrease). A value close to 0 indicates a weak or no

monotonic relationship between the variables. The p-value indicates the statistical significance of the correlation coefficient. If the p-value is less than the chosen significance level (e.g., 0.05), the correlation is considered statistically significant.

How to measure the linear relationship between two continuous variables to predict the value of a dependent variable based on the value of an independent variable?

Measure the linear relationship between Thyroid Stimulating Hormone (TSH) level and Fasting Blood Sugar (FBS) level.

To measure the linear relationship between two continuous variables and predict the value of a dependent variable based on the value of an independent variable, you can use simple linear regression analysis.

1. Launch SPSS and open the dataset containing the TSH level and Fasting Blood Sugar (FBS) level values.
2. Go to the "Analyse" menu at the top of the SPSS window.
3. From the "Analyse" menu, select "Regression" and then click on "Linear."
4. In the "Linear Regression" dialog box, move the FBS level variable to the "Dependent" box. Move the TSH level variable to the "Independent" box.
5. Click the "OK" button to run the linear regression analysis.
6. SPSS will generate output showing the regression coefficients, including the slope (B) and intercept (constant) values. The slope coefficient (B) represents the change in the dependent variable (FBS level) for a one-unit change in the independent variable (TSH level). The intercept represents the value of the dependent variable (FBS level) when the independent variable (TSH level) is zero. The regression equation is in the form: $Y = a + bX$, where Y is the predicted value of the dependent variable (FBS level), X is the value of the independent variable (TSH level), 'a' is the intercept, and 'b' is the slope coefficient.

You can use this equation to predict the FBS level for a given TSH level. Additionally, the output will include the coefficient of determination (R-squared), which indicates the proportion of variance in the dependent variable explained by the independent variable. A higher R-squared value indicates a better fit of the regression model to the data.

How to measure the linear relationship between two continuous variables to predict the value of a dependent variable based on the value of more than one independent variable?

Measure the linear relationship to predict Total cholesterol based on Body Mass Ind (BMI) and Physical activity.

To measure the linear relationship between two continuous variables (BMI and Physical activity) to predict the value of a dependent variable (Total cholesterol) you can perform multiple linear regression analysis.

1. Launch SPSS and load your dataset containing the variables Total cholesterol, BMI, and Physical activity.
2. Ensure that Total cholesterol is set as the dependent variable and BMI and Physical activity are set as independent variables in your dataset.
3. Run Multiple Linear Regression Analysis:

    a) Go to "Analyse" in the top menu.
    b) Select "Regression" and then "Linear..."
    c) In the Linear Regression dialog box:

        i. Move the dependent variable (Total cholesterol) into the "Dependent" box.
        ii. Move the independent variables (BMI and Physical activity) into the "Independent(s)" box.
        iii. Optionally, you can click on "Statistics" to request additional statistics such as coefficients, R-squared, etc.

    d) Click "OK" to run the analysis.

4. The output will include coefficients for each independent variable (BMI and Physical activity), indicating the strength and direction of

their relationship with the dependent variable (Total cholesterol). Look for the significance level (p-value) associated with each coefficient. A low p-value (< 0.05) suggests that the variable is significantly related to the dependent variable. Check the R-squared value to understand the proportion of variance in Total cholesterol explained by the independent variables.

5. You can create scatterplots of Total cholesterol against each independent variable (BMI and Physical activity) to visually inspect the relationship.

6. If you want to predict Total cholesterol for new cases, you can use the coefficients obtained from the regression analysis to compute predicted values based on specific values of BMI and Physical activity.

How to measure the relationship between two or more categorical variables to predict the value of a categorical variable?

Measure the relationship to predict risk factors such as BMI and Physical activity associated with the presence or absence of Diabetes mellitus.

To measure the relationship between two or more categorical variables to predict the value of a categorical variable (such as the presence or absence of Diabetes mellitus) using logistic regression analysis.

1. Make sure your data is properly formatted in SPSS with the variables you need. In this case, you should have variables for BMI, Physical activity, and the presence or absence of Diabetes mellitus (coded as 1 for presence and 0 for absence).

2. Run Logistic Regression Analysis:

    a) Go to "Analyse" in the top menu.

    b) Select "Regression" and then "Binary Logistic..."

    c) In the Binary Logistic Regression dialog box:

        i. Move the dependent variable (presence or absence of Diabetes mellitus) into the "Dependent" box.

        ii. Move the independent variables (BMI and Physical activity) into the "Covariates" box.

    iii. Optionally, you can click on "Categorical" to define any categorical independent variables.

    iv. Click "OK" to run the analysis.

3. The output will include coefficients for each independent variable (BMI and Physical activity), indicating the strength and direction of their relationship with the presence or absence of Diabetes mellitus. Look for the significance level (p-value) associated with each coefficient. A low p-value (< 0.05) suggests that the variable is significantly related to the presence or absence of Diabetes mellitus. Examine the odds ratios associated with each independent variable. Odds ratios indicate the change in odds of having Diabetes mellitus associated with a one-unit change in each predictor variable.

4. Assess the overall fit of the model using goodness-of-fit tests such as the Hosmer-Lemeshow test or the Omnibus test of model coefficients. These tests evaluate how well the model predicts the observed outcomes. Evaluate the classification table to see how well the model predicts the presence or absence of Diabetes mellitus based on the independent variables.

5. You can create graphs or charts to visualise the relationship between the independent variables (BMI, Physical activity) and the presence or absence of Diabetes mellitus.

6. If you want to predict the presence or absence of Diabetes mellitus for new cases, you can use the coefficients obtained from the logistic regression analysis to compute predicted probabilities based on specific values of BMI and Physical activity.

Chapter 11

Questionnaire Designing for Research

A questionnaire is a structured tool used in research to gather data by asking questions to respondents. It is a systematic way to collect information about various aspects of a particular topic or issue of interest. Questionnaires can be administered in different formats, including paper-based forms, online surveys, or face-to-face interviews, depending on the research design and objectives. A good questionnaire must have following characteristics –

1. **Clear and Concise**: Questions should be easy to understand, avoiding jargon or technical language. They should be brief and to the point.

2. **Relevant to Research Objectives**: Each question should directly relate to the research objectives, ensuring that the collected data is useful and meaningful.

3. **Structured and Organized**: The questionnaire should have a logical flow, with questions arranged in a coherent sequence. Grouping related questions together can help maintain consistency and improve respondent engagement.

4. **Unbiased and Neutral**: Questions should be phrased in an unbiased manner to avoid leading respondents to a particular answer. Neutral language ensures the integrity of the data collected.

5. **Multiple Response Options**: Providing multiple response options, including checkboxes, Likert scales, or open-ended fields, allows for flexibility and captures a wider range of responses.

6. **Pre-tested and Validated**: Before deployment, the questionnaire should undergo pre-testing to identify any ambiguities or comprehension issues. Validation ensures that the questionnaire measures what it intends to measure reliably and accurately.

7. **Flexible and Adaptable**: A good questionnaire should be adaptable to different settings and target populations. It should accommodate variations in respondent demographics or cultural backgrounds.

8. **User-friendly Layout**: The questionnaire should be visually appealing and easy to navigate, with clear instructions and formatting.

The key uses of questionnaires in medical research are.

1. **Data Collection**: Questionnaires are commonly used to collect data on various aspects of health, including medical history, symptoms, lifestyle factors, and treatment outcomes. They provide a standardized way of gathering information from participants, ensuring consistency in data collection across different individuals or groups.

2. **Epidemiological Studies**: Questionnaires are essential tools for conducting epidemiological studies to investigate the distribution and determinants of diseases within populations. Researchers use questionnaires to collect data on risk factors, disease prevalence, incidence rates, and patterns of disease occurrence, helping to identify trends and factors contributing to disease development.

3. **Clinical Trials**: In clinical research, questionnaires are used to assess the effectiveness and safety of medical interventions, such as drugs, therapies, or medical devices. Participants may complete questionnaires to report symptoms, treatment adherence, quality of life, and other relevant outcomes, providing valuable data for evaluating the efficacy and impact of interventions.

4. **Patient-reported Outcomes**: Questionnaires enable researchers to capture patient-reported outcomes (PROs), which are measures of health status or quality of life directly reported by patients themselves. PRO questionnaires assess various domains, including physical functioning, emotional well-being, symptom severity, and treatment satisfaction, allowing researchers to evaluate the patient's perspective on their health and treatment experiences.

5. **Health Behaviour Research**: Questionnaires are used to investigate health-related behaviours and lifestyle factors that influence disease risk and health outcomes. Researchers use questionnaires to assess dietary habits, physical activity levels, smoking status,

alcohol consumption, and other behavioural factors, helping to understand the impact of lifestyle choices on health and disease prevention.

6. **Needs Assessment and Health Services Research**: Questionnaires are utilized to assess the healthcare needs and preferences of populations, as well as to evaluate healthcare services and programs. Researchers use questionnaires to gather feedback from patients, healthcare providers, and stakeholders on healthcare delivery, accessibility, satisfaction with services, and areas for improvement.

7. **Screening and Diagnostic Tools**: Questionnaires serve as screening tools for identifying individuals at risk of certain health conditions or mental health disorders. Screening questionnaires, such as depression or anxiety scales, help healthcare professionals detect symptoms or risk factors early, enabling timely intervention and treatment.

8. **Surveys and Population Studies**: Questionnaires are used in population-based surveys and studies to collect data on health-related topics at a larger scale. Surveys may cover a wide range of health issues, including health behaviours, chronic diseases, healthcare utilization, preventive practices, and healthcare access, providing valuable insights into the health status and needs of communities.

Merits of Questionnaires are –

1. **Efficiency**: Questionnaires enable researchers to collect data from a large number of respondents simultaneously, saving time and resources compared to other data collection methods.

2. **Standardisation**: Standardized questionnaires ensure consistency in data collection, reducing the potential for interviewer bias and enhancing reliability.

3. **Anonymity and Confidentiality**: Respondents may feel more comfortable providing honest and candid responses to sensitive or personal questions in a self-administered questionnaire, maintaining anonymity and confidentiality.

4. **Scalability**: Questionnaires can be easily replicated and distributed across different populations or settings, making them suitable for large-scale studies.

5. **Quantification**: Quantitative data collected through questionnaires allow for statistical analysis, enabling researchers to identify patterns, correlations, and associations between variables.

6. **Accessibility**: With advancements in technology, online surveys and electronic questionnaires have increased accessibility, reaching geographically dispersed or hard-to-reach populations.

Demerits of Questionnaires are.

1. **Low Response Rates**: Some respondents may choose not to participate, leading to potential selection bias and reduced generalisability of findings.

2. **Limited Depth of Information**: Questionnaires may provide limited depth or detail compared to other qualitative research methods such as interviews or focus groups, restricting the exploration of complex issues.

3. **Social Desirability Bias**: Respondents may provide socially desirable or exaggerated responses, particularly for sensitive topics, leading to biased results.

4. **Misinterpretation of Questions**: Ambiguous or poorly worded questions may lead to misinterpretation or misunderstanding among respondents, affecting the accuracy of responses.

5. **Sampling Bias**: Questionnaires may not reach certain segments of the population, leading to sampling bias and potentially skewing the results.

6. **Lack of Flexibility**: Once deployed, questionnaires cannot easily adapt to unexpected findings or emerging research questions, limiting flexibility in data collection.

Essential steps for developing a good questionnaire

1. **Define the Research Objectives**: The first step in developing a questionnaire is to clearly define the research objectives. What specific information are you seeking to gather? What research questions or hypotheses do you aim to address? By clearly articulating the research objectives, you can ensure that the questionnaire is focused and aligned with the goals of the study.

2. **Review Existing Literature**: Before designing the questionnaire, it is essential to conduct a thorough review of existing literature related to the research topic. This literature review helps identify relevant concepts, theories, and previous findings that can inform the development of questionnaire items. It also ensures that the questionnaire addresses gaps in knowledge and builds upon existing research.

3. **Identify the Target Population**: Consider the characteristics of the target population for your study, including demographic factors such as age, gender, education level, and socioeconomic status. Understanding the characteristics of the target population helps tailor the questionnaire to the specific needs and preferences of respondents. It also ensures that the questionnaire is relevant and appropriate for the intended audience.

4. **Select an Appropriate Questionnaire Format**: There are several formats for designing questionnaires, including structured (closed-ended), semi-structured, and unstructured (open-ended) formats. Choose the format that best suits the research objectives and the type of data you wish to collect. Structured questionnaires are suitable for gathering quantitative data, while semi-structured and unstructured formats allow for more in-depth exploration of respondents' perspectives.

5. **Develop Questionnaire Items**: Based on the research objectives and literature review, generate a pool of potential questionnaire items or questions that address the key constructs or variables of interest. Ensure that the items are clear, concise, and unambiguous, using language that is easily understandable to the target population. Avoid leading or biased questions that may influence respondents' answers.

6. **Organise Questionnaire Sections**: Organize the questionnaire into logical sections or themes based on the topics or constructs being measured. Group related items together to facilitate respondent comprehension and flow. Consider including introductory sections to provide context and instructions for completing the questionnaire. Pay attention to the sequencing of questions to maintain coherence and minimise respondent fatigue.

7. **Pilot Test the Questionnaire**: Before finalizing the questionnaire, conduct a pilot test with a small sample of representative respondents to evaluate its clarity, comprehensibility, and appropriateness. Solicit feedback from pilot participants regarding the wording of questions, response options, layout, and overall usability of the questionnaire. Use this feedback to refine and improve the questionnaire before administering it to the full sample.

8. **Revise and Finalise the Questionnaire**: Based on the feedback received during the pilot test, revise the questionnaire as needed to address any issues or concerns identified. Ensure that the questionnaire is clear, concise, and free of errors. Finalize the questionnaire for use in the main study, incorporating any necessary revisions or refinements.

9. **Consider Ethical Considerations**: Ensure that the questionnaire adheres to ethical principles, including informed consent, confidentiality, and privacy protections. Obtain necessary ethical approvals or permissions from relevant authorities before administering the questionnaire to participants. Respect participants' rights and ensure that their participation is voluntary and informed.

10. **Pretest the Final Questionnaire**: Conduct a final pretest of the revised questionnaire to verify its clarity, comprehensibility, and appropriateness before administering it to the full sample. Make any final adjustments or refinements as needed based on pretest feedback. Once you are satisfied with the questionnaire, it is ready for use in the main study.

When conducting health research, questionnaires serve as valuable tools for collecting data from participants. These questionnaires can vary in their design and format, depending on the specific objectives of the study, the nature of the research questions, and the characteristics of the target population. The types of questionnaires and response formats commonly used in health research are –

1. **Structured Questionnaires**: Structured questionnaires consist of fixed-response questions with predefined answer choices. They are commonly used in health research to gather quantitative data efficiently. Structured questionnaires allow for standardized data

collection and facilitate statistical analysis. Examples of structured questionnaires include:

Example: The Short Form Health Survey (SF-36) is a structured questionnaire commonly used to assess health-related quality of life. It consists of 36 items covering eight domains, including physical functioning, role limitations due to physical health, bodily pain, general health perceptions, vitality, social functioning, role limitations due to emotional problems, and mental health. Respondents select from predefined response options for each item, such as "Yes/No" or Likert scale ratings.

2. **Semi-Structured Questionnaires**: Semi-structured questionnaires combine fixed-response questions with open-ended questions that allow respondents to provide additional comments or explanations. They offer flexibility in data collection by enabling researchers to explore topics in more depth while still maintaining some standardization. Examples of semi-structured questionnaires include:

   Example: A semi-structured questionnaire on dietary habits may include fixed-response questions about the frequency of consuming specific food groups (e.g., fruits, vegetables, fast food) and open-ended questions asking respondents to describe their typical daily meals or any dietary preferences or restrictions they have.

3. **Unstructured Questionnaires**: Unstructured questionnaires consist primarily of open-ended questions that allow respondents to provide free-form responses without predefined answer choices. They are often used in qualitative research to explore complex topics and capture diverse perspectives. Examples of unstructured questionnaires include:

   Example: An unstructured questionnaire exploring patient experiences with chronic illness management may include open-ended questions asking respondents to describe their experiences living with the condition, the challenges they face, their coping strategies, and their interactions with healthcare providers.

4. **Mixed-Methods Questionnaires**: Mixed-methods questionnaires combine elements of structured, semi-structured, and unstructured

formats to gather both quantitative and qualitative data. They provide a comprehensive approach to data collection, allowing researchers to explore research questions from multiple perspectives. Examples of mixed-methods questionnaires include:

Example: A mixed-methods questionnaire on physical activity and mental health may include structured questions assessing the frequency and intensity of exercise (quantitative data) alongside semi-structured or open-ended questions asking respondents to describe how physical activity impacts their mood and well-being (qualitative data).

Response Formats:

1. **Multiple Choice**: Multiple-choice questions present respondents with a list of predefined answer choices, and they are asked to select the option that best applies to them. Multiple-choice questions are commonly used in structured questionnaires to gather quantitative data efficiently.

   Example,
   Question: How often do you engage in moderate-intensity physical activity?
   A. Never B. Rarely C. Sometimes D. Often E. Always

2. **Likert Scale**: Likert scale questions ask respondents to indicate their level of agreement or disagreement with a statement using a numerical scale. Likert scales are widely used in health research to assess attitudes, perceptions, and preferences.

   Example,
   Question: Please indicate your level of agreement with the following statement: "I feel confident in my ability to manage my chronic illness."

   1. Strongly Disagree
   2. Disagree
   3. Neutral
   4. Agree
   5. Strongly Agree

3. **Numeric Rating Scale**: Numeric rating scales ask respondents to rate their experiences or perceptions using a numerical scale. Numeric rating scales are often used to assess pain intensity, satisfaction levels, or other subjective experiences.

   Example,

   Question: On a scale from 0 to 10, with 0 being no pain and 10 being the worst pain imaginable, please rate your current level of pain.

4. **Ranking Scale**: Ranking scales require respondents to rank items or options in order of preference or importance. Ranking scales are useful for prioritizing choices or identifying preferences among multiple options.

   Example,

   Question: Please rank the following factors in order of importance for maintaining a healthy lifestyle:

   1. Regular exercise
   2. Balanced diet
   3. Sufficient sleep
   4. Stress management.
   5. Avoiding unhealthy habits

5. **Open-Ended**: Open-ended questions allow respondents to provide free-form responses without predefined answer choices. Open-ended questions are commonly used to gather qualitative data and explore complex topics in more depth.

   Example,

   Question: Please describe your experience living with [chronic condition]. What challenges have you faced, and how do you cope with them?

6. **Visual Analog Scale (VAS)**: Visual analog scales ask respondents to mark their response on a continuous line or scale, typically ranging from one extreme to another. Visual analog scales are often used to assess subjective experiences such as pain intensity or mood.
   Example,

Question: Please indicate your current level of fatigue by placing a mark on the line below, where 0 represents "no fatigue" and 10 represents "extreme fatigue."

Understanding Reliability and Validity in Questionnaire Development:

Reliability and validity are crucial aspects of questionnaire design in research. They ensure that the questionnaire consistently measures what it intends to measure and produces accurate and dependable results.

Reliability:

Reliability refers to the consistency and stability of the measurements obtained from a questionnaire. In other words, a reliable questionnaire should yield similar results when administered to the same individuals under similar conditions. There are several types of reliability that researchers commonly assess:

Internal Consistency Reliability: Internal consistency reliability evaluates the extent to which the items within a questionnaire are correlated with each other. One commonly used measure of internal consistency is Cronbach's alpha coefficient, which assesses the interrelatedness of items and indicates how well they form a coherent scale. For example, a researcher may use Cronbach's alpha to assess the internal consistency of a depression scale questionnaire by examining the correlations between different items measuring depression symptoms.

Performing a reliability test using **Cronbach's alpha coefficient** in SPSS, involves following steps –

1. Ensure that the collected responses to a set of items or questions that are intended to measure the same underlying construct. These items should be designed to assess a specific trait, characteristic, or dimension.
2. Input the data into SPSS. Each row represents a participant, and each column represents a response to an item in the questionnaire.
3. Before calculating Cronbach's alpha, it is essential to compute basic descriptive statistics for each item, such as means, standard

deviations, and item-total correlations. This step can provide insights into the distribution and variability of responses.

4. Perform Cronbach's Alpha Analysis in SPSS:

   - Go to "Analyse" in the top menu.
   - Select "Scale" and then "Reliability Analysis..."
   - In the Reliability Analysis dialog box:

     - Move the items that you want to include in the reliability test into the "Items" box.
     - Click on "Statistics" to select the desired statistics (e.g., item statistics, scale if item deleted).
     - Click on "OK" to run the analysis.

The output will include Cronbach's alpha coefficient, indicating the internal consistency reliability of the scale. Cronbach's alpha coefficient ranges from 0 to 1. Higher values indicate greater internal consistency reliability, with values closer to 1 indicating stronger consistency among the items. A commonly accepted threshold for satisfactory reliability is 0.70 or higher, although the acceptable level may vary depending on the context and purpose of the questionnaire. If Cronbach's alpha is below the acceptable threshold, consider removing or revising items with low item-total correlations or exploring the underlying reasons for poor internal consistency.

Ensure that the items included in the reliability test are conceptually related and measure the same underlying construct. Be cautious when interpreting Cronbach's alpha with small sample sizes, as it may be less reliable. Cronbach's alpha assumes that the items are measured on an interval or ratio scale and that the relationship between items is linear. Ensure that these assumptions are met before interpreting the results.

Test-Retest Reliability: Test-retest reliability assesses the stability of questionnaire scores over time by administering the same questionnaire to the same participants on two separate occasions. A test-retest reliability analysis for a questionnaire is conducted using following steps –

1. Ensure that the questionnaire is designed to measure a specific construct or trait consistently over time. The items in the questionnaire should be relevant and appropriate for the study's objectives.
2. Select a sample of participants who are representative of the population of interest. Administer the questionnaire to these participants on the first occasion (Test 1). Ensure that the participants understand the instructions and complete the questionnaire accurately.
3. Determine the time interval between the first and second administrations of the questionnaire. The time interval can vary depending on the nature of the construct being measured and the research context. Common time intervals range from a few days to several weeks.
4. After the specified time interval has elapsed, administer the same questionnaire to the same participants on the second occasion (Test 2). Ensure that the administration procedures and instructions are consistent with those used during the first administration.
5. Once data from both administrations are collected, calculate the correlation coefficient between the scores obtained on Test 1 and Test 2. The correlation coefficient measures the strength and direction of the relationship between the scores obtained at two different points in time.

   - You can use the Pearson correlation coefficient (r) to assess the strength and direction of the relationship between the scores obtained on Test 1 and Test 2 using SPSS.
   - Go to "Analyse" – > "Correlate" – > "Bivariate".
   - Select the variables representing scores on Test 1 and Test 2.
   - Click "OK" to run the analysis.

A high correlation coefficient (close to +1) indicates strong agreement between the scores obtained on Test 1 and Test 2, suggesting high test-retest reliability. A moderate correlation coefficient suggests moderate agreement between the scores obtained on Test 1 and Test 2. A low correlation coefficient (close to 0) indicates poor agreement between the scores obtained on Test 1 and Test 2, suggesting low test-retest reliability.

Inter-Rater Reliability: Inter-rater reliability examines the consistency of questionnaire scores when administered by different raters or observers. This type of reliability is commonly assessed in observational studies or when multiple raters are involved in scoring questionnaire responses. The inter – rater reliability test is conducted by following steps –

1. Ensure that the questionnaire contains items or questions that require scoring or rating by multiple raters or observers. These items should be relevant to the study's objectives and should be clearly defined to minimise ambiguity.

2. Identify and recruit a group of raters or observers who are qualified and competent to score or rate the questionnaire responses. Raters should have adequate training and familiarity with the questionnaire items and scoring criteria.

3. Provide training to the selected raters or observers to ensure consistency and standardization in scoring procedures. Review the questionnaire items, scoring instructions, and any relevant guidelines or protocols with the raters. Conduct practice sessions or calibration exercises to familiarize raters with the scoring process and address any discrepancies or questions.

4. Administer the questionnaire to the participants or subjects included in the study. Ensure that the participants understand the instructions and complete the questionnaire accurately. Collect the questionnaire responses from all participants for scoring by the raters.

5. Instruct the raters to independently score or rate the questionnaire responses according to the established criteria or scoring guidelines. Ensure that each rater evaluates the responses independently and without consulting other raters.

6. Once all raters have completed scoring the questionnaire responses, calculate the inter-rater agreement statistics to assess the consistency of ratings across different raters. Commonly used measures of inter-rater agreement include:

   - **Intraclass Correlation Coefficient (ICC)**: ICC assesses the consistency and agreement among multiple raters' scores. It is commonly used when the scores are continuous or ordinal. ICC can be calculated using SPSS.

1. Navigate to "Analyse" – > "Scale" – > "Reliability Analysis".
2. Move the variables representing scores from different raters into the "Variables" box.
3. Select the desired ICC model under "Model" (e.g., ICC(3,1) for a two-way mixed effect model).
4. Click "Statistics" to specify the desired statistics (e.g., "Scale if item deleted").
5. Click "Continue" and then "OK" to run the analysis.

The ICC value ranges from 0 to 1, where 0 indicates no agreement and 1 indicates perfect agreement among raters. A higher ICC value indicates greater consistency and agreement among raters' scores.

- **Cohen's Kappa Coefficient**: Cohen's Kappa assesses the agreement between two or more raters' categorical or nominal ratings. It corrects for chance agreement and is suitable for dichotomous or categorical data. Cohen's Kappa coefficient can be calculated using SPSS.

  1. Navigate to "Analyse" – > "Descriptive Statistics" – > "Crosstabs".
  2. Select the variables representing ratings from different raters as the row and column variables.
  3. Click on "Statistics" and check the box for "Kappa" under "Kappa and Kendall's tau-b".
  4. Click "Continue" and then "OK" to run the analysis.

  The Cohen's Kappa coefficient value ranges from – 1 to 1. A positive value indicates agreement between raters beyond chance, while a negative value indicates agreement less than chance. A Kappa value of 0 suggests agreement equal to chance.

- **Percent Agreement**: Percent agreement simply calculates the percentage of agreement between raters' scores without correcting for chance agreement. It is a straightforward measure of agreement but may be influenced by prevalence and bias.

Validity

Validity testing of a questionnaire refers to the process of assessing whether the questionnaire measures what it intends to measure. It involves examining the extent to which the questionnaire accurately captures the construct or concept of interest. There are several types of validity that researchers commonly assess:

1. **Content Validity**: Content validity refers to the extent to which the items in a questionnaire represent the entire domain or content of the construct being measured. It involves evaluating whether the questionnaire items adequately cover all relevant aspects of the construct. Content validity is typically established through expert judgment, content analysis, and qualitative methods.
   1. Generate a pool of initial items or questions that you believe are relevant to the construct based on your understanding and review of existing literature. These items should reflect different aspects or dimensions of the construct and cover a broad range of content.
   2. Identify a panel of experts who are knowledgeable and experienced in the field relevant to the construct being measured. Experts may include researchers, practitioners, or professionals with expertise in the subject area. Aim for diversity in expertise and perspectives to ensure comprehensive coverage of the construct.
   3. Present the pool of initial items to the panel of experts for review. Ask the experts to evaluate each item based on its relevance, clarity, and representativeness of the construct. Encourage experts to provide feedback on whether any important aspects of the construct are missing or underrepresented.
   4. Calculate the Content Validity Index (CVI) to quantify the extent to which the items in the questionnaire are considered relevant and representative by the panel of experts. CVI is typically calculated as the proportion of items rated as relevant or representative by the experts.
   5. CVI = Number of items rated as relevant or representative / Total number of items

6. Establish a threshold for acceptable content validity based on the CVI scores. A commonly used threshold is 0.80, meaning that at least 80% of the items should be rated as relevant or representative by the experts to demonstrate adequate content validity. However, the threshold may vary depending on the context and purpose of the questionnaire.

7. Review the feedback from the experts and revise the questionnaire items as needed. Remove irrelevant or redundant items, clarify ambiguous wording, and add missing items to ensure comprehensive coverage of the construct. Repeat the content validity assessment if significant changes are made to the questionnaire.

2. **Criterion Validity**: Criterion validity assesses the extent to which scores on a questionnaire correlate with scores on an established criterion measure of the same construct. There are two subtypes of criterion validity:

- **Concurrent Validity**: Concurrent validity evaluates the correlation between scores on the questionnaire and scores on a criterion measure administered concurrently. For example, a researcher may administer a new depression questionnaire to patients and compare their scores with scores on a well-established depression scale administered at the same time.

- **Predictive Validity**: Predictive validity evaluates the extent to which scores on the questionnaire predict future performance or outcomes on a criterion measure. For instance, a researcher may administer a questionnaire measuring risk factors for cardiovascular disease to a group of participants and then track their health outcomes (e.g., incidence of heart disease) over several years to determine whether the questionnaire scores predict future risk.

3. **Construct Validity**: Construct validity assesses the degree to which scores on a questionnaire correspond with theoretical constructs or concepts related to the measured construct. It involves testing hypotheses about the relationships between the questionnaire scores

and other variables. Construct validity can be established through convergent validity, discriminant validity, and factor analysis. For example, a researcher may administer a questionnaire measuring job satisfaction and examine its correlations with related constructs such as job performance, organizational commitment, and turnover intentions to establish construct validity.

4. **Face Validity**: Face validity refers to the extent to which a questionnaire appears to measure what it is intended to measure based on face value or superficial assessment. It involves examining whether the questionnaire items are clear, relevant, and appropriate to the construct being measured. While face validity does not provide strong evidence of validity, it is useful for gauging respondents' perceptions of the questionnaire's relevance and acceptability.

5. **Consequential Validity**: Consequential validity assesses the potential consequences or impacts of using the questionnaire in practice. It involves evaluating whether the questionnaire produces meaningful and desirable outcomes when used for its intended purpose. This type of validity considers the broader implications of using the questionnaire in decision-making, policy development, or program evaluation.

Chapter 12

Ethical Considerations in Statistical Analysis for Medical Research

Medical research plays a pivotal role in advancing our understanding of diseases, developing new treatments, and improving patient outcomes. Statistical analysis serves as a fundamental tool in medical research, enabling researchers to analyse data, draw conclusions, and make evidence-based decisions. However, the use of statistical methods in medical research raises several ethical considerations that must be carefully addressed to ensure the integrity, validity, and ethical conduct of research studies. This essay explores the ethical considerations associated with statistical analysis in medical research, highlighting the importance of upholding ethical principles to safeguard the rights and welfare of research participants and maintain public trust in research findings.

Ethical Principles in Medical Research

Before delving into the specific ethical considerations related to statistical analysis, it is essential to understand the foundational ethical principles that guide research involving human participants. These principles include:

- **Respect for Persons**: Researchers must respect the autonomy and dignity of research participants, ensuring that individuals have the right to make informed decisions about their participation in research studies.
- **Beneficence**: Researchers have a duty to maximize benefits and minimise harms to research participants, prioritizing their well-being and safety throughout the research process.

- **Justice**: The benefits and burdens of research should be distributed fairly among participants, ensuring that vulnerable populations are not exploited or disproportionately burdened by research activities.
- **Informed Consent**: Informed consent is a cornerstone of ethical research, requiring researchers to provide participants with comprehensive information about the study purpose, procedures, risks, benefits, and alternatives to participation. Participants must voluntarily consent to participate in research after fully understanding the information provided.
- **Privacy and Confidentiality**: Researchers must protect the privacy and confidentiality of research participants, ensuring that sensitive information is safeguarded against unauthorized access or disclosure.

Ethical Considerations in Statistical Analysis

The specific ethical considerations associated with statistical analysis in medical research are

- **Data Privacy and Confidentiality**: Protecting the privacy and confidentiality of research participants' data is paramount in statistical analysis. Researchers must implement appropriate safeguards to prevent unauthorized access, disclosure, or misuse of sensitive information. This includes anonymizing or de-identifying data to minimise the risk of re-identification and ensuring secure storage and transmission of data.
- **Informed Consent and Participant Autonomy**: Statistical analysis often involves the use of data collected from research participants. Researchers must obtain informed consent from participants before collecting, analysing, or sharing their data for research purposes. Participants should be fully informed about how their data will be used, including any potential risks or limitations associated with data sharing and analysis.
- **Transparency and Reproducibility**: Transparency and reproducibility are essential principles in statistical analysis, ensuring that research findings can be independently verified and validated by others. Researchers should provide clear documentation of their

statistical methods, data analysis procedures, and assumptions, allowing others to replicate the results and assess the robustness of the findings. Transparent reporting of statistical analyses enhances the credibility and trustworthiness of research findings.

- **Avoiding Data Manipulation and Misrepresentation**: Researchers must conduct statistical analyses with integrity and honesty, avoiding data manipulation or misrepresentation to achieve desired results. This includes accurately reporting data outliers, handling missing data appropriately, and avoiding selective reporting of statistical tests or analyses to support a particular hypothesis. Misleading or biased statistical analyses undermine the validity and reliability of research findings and erode public trust in scientific research.

- **Conflicts of Interest and Disclosure**: Researchers should disclose any potential conflicts of interest that may influence the design, conduct, or reporting of statistical analyses. Conflicts of interest may arise from financial relationships, professional affiliations, or personal biases that could affect the objectivity and impartiality of research findings. Transparency and disclosure of conflicts of interest are essential for maintaining research integrity and ensuring the credibility of research findings.

Bibliography

1. Altman, D. G. (1991). Practical Statistics for Medical Research. London: Chapman and Hall/CRC.
2. Dawson, B., Trapp, R. G., & Trapp, R. G. (2004). Basic & Clinical Biostatistics. New York: Lange Medical Books/McGraw-Hill.
3. Kirkwood, B. R., & Sterne, J. A. (2003). Essential Medical Statistics. Malden, MA: Blackwell Science.
4. Bland, J. M. (2000). An Introduction to Medical Statistics. Oxford: Oxford University Press.
5. Armitage, P., & Berry, G. (2001). Statistical Methods in Medical Research. Oxford: Blackwell Science.
6. Glantz, S. A. (2011). Primer of Biostatistics (7th ed.). New York: McGraw-Hill Medical.
7. Pagano, M., & Gauvreau, K. (2018). Principles of Biostatistics (3rd ed.). Boston, MA: Cengage Learning.
8. Martin, B. (2008). Understanding Medical Statistics. London: Hodder Arnold.
9. Peat, J., Barton, B., & Elliott, E. (2019). Statistics Workbook for Evidence-Based Health Care. Chichester, West Sussex, UK: Wiley Blackwell.
10. Machin, D., Campbell, M. J., & Walters, S. J. (2007). Medical Statistics: A Textbook for the Health Sciences (4th ed.). Chichester, West Sussex, UK: Wiley-Blackwell.
11. Petrie, A., & Sabin, C. (2009). Medical Statistics at a Glance (3rd ed.). Oxford: Wiley-Blackwell.
12. Szklo, M., & Nieto, F. J. (2014). Epidemiology: Beyond the Basics (4th ed.). Burlington, MA: Jones & Bartlett Learning.
13. Rosner, B. (2015). Fundamentals of Biostatistics (8th ed.). Boston, MA: Cengage Learning.
14. Swinscow, T. D. V., & Campbell, M. J. (2002). Statistics at Square One (9th ed.). London: BMJ Books.

Glossary

1. Biostatistics: The application of statistical methods to biological and medical data.
2. Epidemiology: The study of the distribution and determinants of health-related events in populations and the application of this study to control health problems.
3. Descriptive statistics: Methods used to summarize and describe the main features of a dataset.
4. Inferential statistics: Methods used to make inferences or predictions about a population based on sample data.
5. Population: The entire group of individuals or items of interest in a statistical study.
6. Sample: A subset of the population selected for analysis in a statistical study.
7. Variable: A characteristic or attribute that can take different values.
8. Continuous variable: A variable that can take any value within a range (e.g., height, weight).
9. Discrete variable: A variable that can only take specific, distinct values (e.g., number of children).
10. Independent variable: The variable that is manipulated or controlled by the researcher in an experiment.
11. Dependent variable: The variable that is measured or observed in response to changes in the independent variable.
12. Mean: The average value of a set of numbers calculated by dividing the sum of the values by the total number of values.
13. Median: The middle value of a dataset when the values are arranged in ascending order.
14. Mode: The value that occurs most frequently in a dataset.

15. Standard deviation: A measure of the dispersion or spread of values in a dataset.
16. Confidence interval: A range of values within which the true value of a population parameter is estimated to lie with a certain level of confidence.
17. Hypothesis testing: A statistical method used to determine whether there is enough evidence to reject a null hypothesis.
18. Null hypothesis: A statement that there is no significant difference or relationship between variables.
19. Alternative hypothesis: A statement that there is a significant difference or relationship between variables.
20. p-value: The probability of obtaining the observed results of a statistical test, assuming that the null hypothesis is true.
21. Type I error: Rejecting the null hypothesis when it is actually true (false positive).
22. Type II error: Failing to reject the null hypothesis when it is actually false (false negative).
23. Power: The probability of correctly rejecting a false null hypothesis (1 – Type II error rate).
24. Regression analysis: A statistical method used to examine the relationship between one or more independent variables and a dependent variable.
25. Correlation coefficient: A measure of the strength and direction of the linear relationship between two variables.
26. Odds ratio: A measure of the association between an exposure and an outcome in case-control studies and logistic regression.
27. Risk ratio: A measure of the relative risk or likelihood of an outcome in exposed versus unexposed groups.
28. Survival analysis: A statistical method used to analyse the time until an event of interest occurs (e.g., death, recurrence of disease).
29. Kaplan-Meier estimator: A nonparametric method used to estimate the survival function from censored data.
30. Hazard ratio: A measure of the relative hazard or risk of an event occurring in one group compared to another group in survival analysis.

31. Receiver operating characteristic (ROC) curve: A graphical plot used to assess the performance of a binary classifier system.
32. Sensitivity: The proportion of true positive results correctly identified by a diagnostic test.
33. Specificity: The proportion of true negative results correctly identified by a diagnostic test.
34. Confounding variable: A variable that is associated with both the exposure and outcome of interest, leading to a spurious association.
35. Randomisation: The process of assigning participants to different study groups by chance to reduce bias in experimental studies.
36. Blinding: The practice of keeping study participants, investigators, or outcome assessors unaware of treatment assignments to minimise bias.
37. Cross-sectional study: A type of observational study that examines the relationship between variables at a single point in time.
38. Cohort study: A type of observational study that follows a group of individuals over time to assess the incidence of outcomes.
39. Case-control study: A type of observational study that compares individuals with a specific outcome (cases) to those without the outcome (controls) to identify potential risk factors.
40. Randomised controlled trial (RCT): A type of experimental study in which participants are randomly assigned to different treatment groups to assess the effectiveness of interventions.
41. Intention-to-treat analysis: An analysis approach that includes all participants according to their randomised treatment assignment, regardless of whether they completed the treatment.
42. Per-protocol analysis: An analysis approach that includes only participants who completed the treatment according to the study protocol.
43. Interquartile range (IQR): A measure of statistical dispersion calculated as the difference between the third and first quartiles.
44. Outlier: An observation that is significantly different from other observations in a dataset.
45. Normal distribution: A symmetric, bell-shaped distribution characterized by a mean, median, and mode that are equal.

46. Skewness: A measure of the asymmetry of the distribution of values in a dataset.
47. Kurtosis: A measure of the "tailedness" of the distribution of values in a dataset.
48. Parametric statistics: Statistical methods that make assumptions about the distribution of the data (e.g., normal distribution).
49. Nonparametric statistics: Statistical methods that do not rely on specific assumptions about the distribution of the data.
50. Missing data: Data that are not available or not recorded for some observations in a dataset, which can affect the validity and generalisability of study findings.

Appendix I

t-distribution

					Confidence Level					
	60%	70%	80%	85%	90%	95%	98%	99%	99.8%	99.9%
					Level of Significance					
2 Tailed	0.40	0.30	0.20	0.15	0.10	0.05	0.02	0.01	0.002	0.001
1 Tailed	0.20	0.15	0.10	0.075	0.05	0.025	0.01	0.005	0.001	0.0005
df										
1	1.376	1.963	3.133	4.195	6.320	12.69	31.81	63.67	—	—
2	1.060	1.385	1.883	2.278	2.912	4.271	6.816	9.520	19.65	26.30
3	0.978	1.250	1.637	1.924	2.352	3.179	4.525	5.797	9.937	12.39
4	0.941	1.190	1.533	1.778	2.132	2.776	3.744	4.596	7.115	8.499
5	0.919	1.156	1.476	1.699	2.015	2.570	3.365	4.030	5.876	6.835
6	0.906	1.134	1.440	1.650	1.943	2.447	3.143	3.707	5.201	5.946
7	0.896	1.119	1.415	1.617	1.895	2.365	2.999	3.500	4.783	5.403
8	0.889	1.108	1.397	1.592	1.860	2.306	2.897	3.356	4.500	5.039
9	0.883	1.100	1.383	1.574	1.833	2.262	2.822	3.250	4.297	4.780
10	0.879	1.093	1.372	1.559	1.813	2.228	2.764	3.170	4.144	4.586
11	0.875	1.088	1.363	1.548	1.796	2.201	2.719	3.106	4.025	4.437
12	0.873	1.083	1.356	1.538	1.782	2.179	2.682	3.055	3.930	4.318
13	0.870	1.079	1.350	1.530	1.771	2.160	2.651	3.013	3.852	4.221
14	0.868	1.076	1.345	1.523	1.761	2.145	2.625	2.977	3.788	4.141
15	0.866	1.074	1.341	1.517	1.753	2.131	2.603	2.947	3.733	4.073
16	0.865	1.071	1.337	1.512	1.746	2.120	2.584	2.921	3.687	4.015
17	0.863	1.069	1.333	1.508	1.740	2.110	2.567	2.899	3.646	3.965
18	0.862	1.067	1.330	1.504	1.734	2.101	2.553	2.879	3.611	3.922
19	0.861	1.066	1.328	1.500	1.729	2.093	2.540	2.861	3.580	3.884
20	0.860	1.064	1.325	1.497	1.725	2.086	2.529	2.846	3.552	3.850
21	0.859	1.063	1.323	1.494	1.721	2.080	2.518	2.832	3.528	3.820
22	0.858	1.061	1.321	1.492	1.717	2.074	2.509	2.819	3.505	3.792
23	0.857	1.060	1.319	1.489	1.714	2.069	2.500	2.808	3.485	3.768
24	0.857	1.059	1.318	1.487	1.711	2.064	2.493	2.797	3.467	3.746
25	0.856	1.058	1.316	1.485	1.708	2.060	2.486	2.788	3.451	3.725
26	0.856	1.058	1.315	1.483	1.706	2.056	2.479	2.779	3.435	3.707
27	0.855	1.057	1.314	1.482	1.703	2.052	2.473	2.771	3.421	3.690
28	0.855	1.056	1.313	1.480	1.701	2.048	2.468	2.764	3.409	3.674
29	0.854	1.055	1.311	1.479	1.699	2.045	2.463	2.757	3.397	3.660
30	0.854	1.055	1.310	1.477	1.697	2.042	2.458	2.750	3.386	3.646
40	0.851	1.050	1.303	1.468	1.684	2.021	2.424	2.705	3.307	3.551
50	0.849	1.047	1.299	1.462	1.676	2.009	2.404	2.678	3.262	3.496
60	0.848	1.045	1.296	1.458	1.671	2.000	2.391	2.661	3.232	3.460
70	0.847	1.044	1.294	1.456	1.667	1.994	2.381	2.648	3.211	3.435
80	0.846	1.043	1.292	1.453	1.664	1.990	2.374	2.639	3.196	3.417
90	0.846	1.042	1.291	1.452	1.662	1.987	2.369	2.632	3.184	3.402
100	0.845	1.042	1.290	1.451	1.660	1.984	2.365	2.626	3.174	3.391
∞	0.842	1.036	1.282	1.440	1.645	1.960	2.327	2.576	3.091	3.291

Appendix II

Chi-square Distribution Table

d.f.	.995	.99	.975	.95	.9	.1	.05	.025	.01
1	0.00	0.00	0.00	0.00	0.02	2.71	3.84	5.02	6.63
2	0.01	0.02	0.05	0.10	0.21	4.61	5.99	7.38	9.21
3	0.07	0.11	0.22	0.35	0.58	6.25	7.81	9.35	11.34
4	0.21	0.30	0.48	0.71	1.06	7.78	9.49	11.14	13.28
5	0.41	0.55	0.83	1.15	1.61	9.24	11.07	12.83	15.09
6	0.68	0.87	1.24	1.64	2.20	10.64	12.59	14.45	16.81
7	0.99	1.24	1.69	2.17	2.83	12.02	14.07	16.01	18.48
8	1.34	1.65	2.18	2.73	3.49	13.36	15.51	17.53	20.09
9	1.73	2.09	2.70	3.33	4.17	14.68	16.92	19.02	21.67
10	2.16	2.56	3.25	3.94	4.87	15.99	18.31	20.48	23.21
11	2.60	3.05	3.82	4.57	5.58	17.28	19.68	21.92	24.72
12	3.07	3.57	4.40	5.23	6.30	18.55	21.03	23.34	26.22
13	3.57	4.11	5.01	5.89	7.04	19.81	22.36	24.74	27.69
14	4.07	4.66	5.63	6.57	7.79	21.06	23.68	26.12	29.14
15	4.60	5.23	6.26	7.26	8.55	22.31	25.00	27.49	30.58
16	5.14	5.81	6.91	7.96	9.31	23.54	26.30	28.85	32.00
17	5.70	6.41	7.56	8.67	10.09	24.77	27.59	30.19	33.41
18	6.26	7.01	8.23	9.39	10.86	25.99	28.87	31.53	34.81
19	6.84	7.63	8.91	10.12	11.65	27.20	30.14	32.85	36.19
20	7.43	8.26	9.59	10.85	12.44	28.41	31.41	34.17	37.57
22	8.64	9.54	10.98	12.34	14.04	30.81	33.92	36.78	40.29
24	9.89	10.86	12.40	13.85	15.66	33.20	36.42	39.36	42.98
26	11.16	12.20	13.84	15.38	17.29	35.56	38.89	41.92	45.64
28	12.46	13.56	15.31	16.93	18.94	37.92	41.34	44.46	48.28
30	13.79	14.95	16.79	18.49	20.60	40.26	43.77	46.98	50.89
32	15.13	16.36	18.29	20.07	22.27	42.58	46.19	49.48	53.49
34	16.50	17.79	19.81	21.66	23.95	44.90	48.60	51.97	56.06
38	19.29	20.69	22.88	24.88	27.34	49.51	53.38	56.90	61.16
42	22.14	23.65	26.00	28.14	30.77	54.09	58.12	61.78	66.21
46	25.04	26.66	29.16	31.44	34.22	58.64	62.83	66.62	71.20
50	27.99	29.71	32.36	34.76	37.69	63.17	67.50	71.42	76.15
55	31.73	33.57	36.40	38.96	42.06	68.80	73.31	77.38	82.29
60	35.53	37.48	40.48	43.19	46.46	74.40	79.08	83.30	88.38
65	39.38	41.44	44.60	47.45	50.88	79.97	84.82	89.18	94.42
70	43.28	45.44	48.76	51.74	55.33	85.53	90.53	95.02	100.43
75	47.21	49.48	52.94	56.05	59.79	91.06	96.22	100.84	106.39
80	51.17	53.54	57.15	60.39	64.28	96.58	101.88	106.63	112.33
85	55.17	57.63	61.39	64.75	68.78	102.08	107.52	112.39	118.24
90	59.20	61.75	65.65	69.13	73.29	107.57	113.15	118.14	124.12
95	63.25	65.90	69.92	73.52	77.82	113.04	118.75	123.86	129.97
100	67.33	70.06	74.22	77.93	82.36	118.50	124.34	129.56	135.81

Critical Values for Pearson's Correlation Coefficient

	Proportion in ONE Tail					
	.25	.10	.05	.025	.01	.005
	Proportion in TWO Tails					
DF	.50	.20	.10	.05	.02	.01
1	.7071	.9511	.9877	.9969	.9995	.9999
2	.5000	.8000	.9000	.9500	.9800	.9900
3	.4040	.6870	.8054	.8783	.9343	.9587
4	.3473	.6084	.7293	.8114	.8822	.9172
5	.3091	.5509	.6694	.7545	.8329	.8745
6	.2811	.5067	.6215	.7067	.7887	.8343
7	.2596	.4716	.5822	.6664	.7498	.7977
8	.2423	.4428	.5494	.6319	.7155	.7646
9	.2281	.4187	.5214	.6021	.6851	.7348
10	.2161	.3981	.4973	.5760	.6581	.7079
11	.2058	.3802	.4762	.5529	.6339	.6835
12	.1968	.3646	.4575	.5324	.6120	.6614
13	.1890	.3507	.4409	.5140	.5923	.6411
14	.1820	.3383	.4259	.4973	.5742	.6226
15	.1757	.3271	.4124	.4821	.5577	.6055
16	.1700	.3170	.4000	.4683	.5425	.5897
17	.1649	.3077	.3887	.4555	.5285	.5751
18	.1602	.2992	.3783	.4438	.5155	.5614
19	.1558	.2914	.3687	.4329	.5034	.5487
20	.1518	.2841	.3598	.4227	.4921	.5368
21	.1481	.2774	.3515	.4132	.4815	.5256
22	.1447	.2711	.3438	.4044	.4716	.5151
23	.1415	.2653	.3365	.3961	.4622	.5052
24	.1384	.2598	.3297	.3882	.4534	.4958
25	.1356	.2546	.3233	.3809	.4451	.4869
26	.1330	.2497	.3172	.3739	.4372	.4785
27	.1305	.2451	.3115	.3673	.4297	.4705
28	.1281	.2407	.3061	.3610	.4226	.4629
29	.1258	.2366	.3009	.3550	.4158	.4556
30	.1237	.2327	.2960	.3494	.4093	.4487
31	.1217	.2289	.2913	.3440	.4032	.4421
32	.1197	.2254	.2869	.3388	.3972	.4357
33	.1179	.2220	.2826	.3338	.3916	.4296
34	.1161	.2187	.2785	.3291	.3862	.4238
35	.1144	.2156	.2746	.3246	.3810	.4182
36	.1128	.2126	.2709	.3202	.3760	.4128
37	.1113	.2097	.2673	.3160	.3712	.4076
38	.1098	.2070	.2638	.3120	.3665	.4026
39	.1084	.2043	.2605	.3081	.3621	.3978
40	.1070	.2018	.2573	.3044	.3578	.3932
41	.1057	.1993	.2542	.3008	.3536	.3887
42	.1044	.1970	.2512	.2973	.3496	.3843
43	.1032	.1947	.2483	.2940	.3457	.3801
44	.1020	.1925	.2455	.2907	.3420	.3761
45	.1008	.1903	.2429	.2876	.3384	.3721
46	.0997	.1883	.2403	.2845	.3348	.3683
47	.0987	.1863	.2377	.2816	.3314	.3646
48	.0976	.1843	.2353	.2787	.3281	.3610
49	.0966	.1825	.2329	.2759	.3249	.3575
50	.0956	.1806	.2306	.2732	.3218	.3542